Positivity

Advance Praise for *Positivity*

"Reading *Positivity* is a game changer for every reader. The unique wisdom and philosophy of life that Harry Edelson shares proves that life can be easy and joyful for everyone. Imagine a world if seven billion people lived by *Positivity*! Thank you for sharing this masterpiece. Harry Edelson has figured out true keys to a good life—which is the one common denominator everyone wants. And I know, because I've interviewed over 400 of the top CEOs, and I see a lot of wisdom and very successful people . . . and Harry has truly figured it out. What a gift you offer in this book."

—ROBERT REISS
Host & CEO, *The CEO Show*

"I have enjoyed the book very much. Reading your words puts me in your energy field, which I so appreciate. You are such an inspiration!"

—ROBERT GAMBEE
Author of *Nantucket Island, Wall Street*, and eight other books

"As Benjamin Franklin said: 'An investment in knowledge pays the best interest.' The wisdom in Harry Edelson's book is like finding a great investment. It continues to grow in value and will pay dividends throughout your life. This is the same philosophy that the brilliant investor, George Soros, has advocated through his Open Society Foundations where I served as a trustee for many years."

—JOHN W. ALLEN
Int'l Investment Banker and Chairman of Greater China Corp

"Harry Edelson was a legendary Wall Street securities analyst, a legendary venture capital investor for ten of the largest corporations in the world, and is soon to be a legendary author because *Positivity* will inspire every reader."

—BRIAN S. COHEN
Chairman, New York Angels

"Harry Edelson is so very special and exceptionally inspiring. The contagious energy that Harry conveys incredibly exceeds even that of the most spirited twenty-year-old. I found that his story of an extremely challenging upbringing in (the slums of) East New York and losing his father when while still a baby and, nevertheless, somehow developing on his own to achieve such remarkable entrepreneurial brilliance and a spectacularly amazing career—indeed his whole life—is like an extraordinarily captivating movie."

—J. MORTON DAVIS
Chairman of the Board, D.H. Blair Investment Banking Corp.

"Harry's positivity is both inspiring and infectious. Seeing the impact he had on my students, I invited Harry to participate in the Veterans Entrepreneurship Boot Camp I run at Pace University, confident that these military veterans would find the same inspiration in Harry's positive attitude and boundless enthusiasm. Similar to entrepreneurship, happiness is a mindset—a way of thinking and acting—and *Positivity* is a uniquely valuable resource in understanding how it may be achieved."

—PROF. BRUCE BACHENHEIMER
Executive Director, Entrepreneurship Lab, Pace University

"The interesting thing about Harry Edelson is that he is usually the smartest guy in the room, and what is amazing, the happiest guy in the room. His book tells it all and can be easily absorbed by adults and students alike."

—ELIZABETH KABLER
Trustee, Annenberg Foundation Trust at Sunnylands and Founder,
NY Center for Living

"As a top-ranked research analyst for Merrill Lynch, Drexel Burnham, and First Boston in the 1970s and 1980s, Harry had a front row seat on the tumultuous changes on Wall Street. This, combined with an outstanding career as a venture capitalist over the past 30 years, gives him a unique perspective on the finance industry. This book is a must-read for Millennials looking for advice on careers, personal finances, and life itself."

—GEORGE A. NEEDHAM
Chairman & CEO, The Needham Group, Inc.

Positivity

How to Be Happier, Healthier, Smarter, and More Prosperous

HARRY EDELSON

SelectBooks, Inc.
New York

This edition published by SelectBooks, Inc.
For information address SelectBooks, Inc., New York, New York.

First Edition

ISBN 978-1-59079-355-8

Library of Congress Cataloging-in-Publication Data
Edelson, Harry.
 Positivity : how to be happier, healthier, smarter, and more prosperous /
Harry Edelson. -- First Edition.
     pages cm
 Summary: "Successful entrepreneur as advisor and consultant for strategic
venture capital investments of leading technology corporations, tells his
story of rising from poverty to great prosperity. He gives advice on how to
achieve emotional and physical well-being and financial success though
positive attitudes, continual improvement of education and skills, and a
lifelong willingness to learn something new"-- Provided by publisher.
 ISBN 978-1-59079-355-8 (hardbound book : alk. paper) 1. Attitude
(Psychology) 2. Happiness. 3. Success. I. Title.
 BF327.E34 2015
 158--dc23
                                        2015004390

Book design by Janice Benight
Illustration page 160 © Joyce Mirhan Turley

Manufactured in the United States of America
10 9 8 7 6 5 4 3 2 1

Dedicated to the thousands of people who have asked me
to write a book that would provide inspiration and guidance
to lead lives of happiness.

CONTENTS

Part Three

Be Smarter 91

Part Four

Be More Prosperous 147

Foreword

I HAVE KNOWN HARRY EDELSON for many years, and he has always been happy and energetic with a mind that is always acute. He has spoken extemporaneously and in good humor to large groups of my clients on a variety of subjects with nary an um or an uh.

Yet I began reading *Positivity: How to be Happier, Healthier, Smarter, and More Prosperous* with a good deal of skepticism. "How to Be Happy" books are often rich with hope and poor on utility.

Some of the chapters seemed at first unrelated: Why are we learning investment strategy, memory enhancing techniques, reading skills, and the power of positive thinking all in one book? While the English Teacher in me thought this, I decided that Harry Edelson had explained this very well—because Healthy, Smart, and Prosperous people are, in fact, happier people. I think the recommendations for skill building in each of these sections is therefore most useful.

I finished reading *Positivity* with new ideas noted, some game plans for making changes in how I do things, and with great respect for the author and my friend Harry Edelson.

I appreciated the humor and anecdotes that Harry Edelson weaves through the chapters. I like that he shares his own personal life and the "commandments" to himself. I like that he challenges underlying assumptions regardless of the pedigree from which they originate.

An excellent way to evaluate anything we read or hear is to ask ourselves if the experience left us feeling enriched. Gaining one new concept does the trick for me. But *Positivity* left me richer by over twenty concepts I would like to implement.

The author's simple desire is to make us better at who we already are. There is not anyone who could read this book and not walk away with a better idea.

—Pamela J. Newman, PhD
Aon plc
President & CEO, Newman Team

Preface

WHILE GIVING KEYNOTE SPEECHES at numerous conferences throughout the world, at least 1,000 attendees inspired by my energetic presentations have approached me afterwards and urged me to write a book about my attitude, activities, energy, and joie de vivre. Requests to write a book come from the young and old, business people and educators. When I asked them why I should write a book, they answered that they want to be as happy, healthy, and successful as I am. I listened and the result is this book.

In it I reveal my secrets for achieving perpetual happiness, excellent health, the best skills for learning, and—finally—how to save and invest money to become financially independent and secure. My bag of tricks includes practical and simple methods to read faster, comprehend more, and do mental math.

Applying skills and lessons that I learned from reading books and attending lectures resulted in my service on over one hundred twenty-five boards, as an investor in more than one hundred fifty companies, and a career in finance and technology at ten huge corporations and dozens of emerging growth companies.

Be my guest! Gain from my experience and open yourself to possibilities that will change your life for the better. What I learned, you can learn; it is that easy. The four parts of this book build on each other and blend together as a recipe for achieving success and happiness. With the inspiration and knowledge you can gain from each chapter, you can become what the four divisions of my book indicate were my goals: to be happier, healthier, smarter, and more prosperous.

Consider this: if you are not taking care of your health, not getting smarter by reading to learn more, not presenting yourself better and obtaining the best job available, and not making money and saving properly, how the heck are you going to be happy? The book progresses to explain this in a systematic way, but the reader may choose to read any part of the book out of order.

You, like me, can be as happy as you want to be. If you are happy you are more likely to be healthy, as every doctor will tell you. I am happy and healthy 100 percent of the time. One of the topics discussed is the placebo effect and the nocebo effect which provide powerful proof that the mind affects your health. I maintain that positive reinforcement by doctors, family, or friends will also contribute to making you happier and healthier.

Another powerful influence on my happiness and success occurred years ago when I attended an Evelyn Wood Reading Dynamics® class and discovered that I could read 4,000 words per minute with excellent comprehension. In this age of accelerating technology, there are simple ways to increase your reading speed in order to stay on top of these new influences in your life.

I will show you how to read a list of one hundred items in any order and in twenty minutes repeat them back perfectly regardless of the order. You will never again need to make a shopping list! There is even a system to remember 10,000 things in any order, which I will describe, but who really needs to remember 10,000 things?

With the techniques I provide, you will be able to deliver a speech of thirty minutes to a large audience without notes and with little preparation. You will eliminate the fear of public speaking and learn the secrets to making an exciting presentation at any time.

There are also many simple tricks of mathematics that can be learned in a short time. Do not be afraid of math. Math is fun, as I will explain. For example, you can square a two-digit number ending in five instantaneously and can multiply two-digit numbers such as 88×95 in your head in seconds.

Saving money can be just as important as making money, as per the old adage often attributed to Benjamin Franklin, "A penny saved is a penny earned." You need to be conscious of your budget, eliminate impulse buying, and shop wisely.

There are smart ways to invest, and there are dumb ways to invest. I will provide you with an almost foolproof method of investing money wisely by employing the powerful tools of compound interest, dollar cost averaging, and indexing. Becoming financially independent will give you tremendous confidence and freedom from stress.

The average person can learn to do all of these things and more by following the advice provided in this book. Open your mind to the possibilities of achieving a happiness and success you never thought possible. You are never too poor, too old, too intelligent, or too comfortable to learn new tricks.

Introduction

I GREW UP IN THE POOREST NEIGHBORHOOD in Brooklyn, which was the poorest neighborhood in New York City, and I was the poorest of the poor. To me, the greatest technology known to mankind was the radio, recently invented. Horses in the streets were common, but automobiles were on their way. I did not know my rear end from my elbow, but based on test scores and having skipped a grade, my teachers at Junior High School 109 in Brownsville enrolled me in Brooklyn Technical High School. The only tools I knew, but not very well, were a hammer and a screwdriver. I was not allowed to drive a nail into the walls of my tenement because the landlord could charge us for the damage to the wall.

Here I was at Brooklyn Technical High School being introduced to such things as lathes and foundries that actually made things. My fellow students talked about things I had never heard of or paid attention to—things like centimeters and micrometers, concepts way beyond my comprehension. How bewildering. I traveled thirty minutes by subway to go to school each day while my friends happily played ball in the street and attended Thomas Jefferson High School, only a few blocks from my tenement. What a schmuck I was. How ironic is it that I became one of the best-known technology experts in the world?

What motivated me to write this book? First, the accelerating impact of technology has changed our lives irrevocably. Second, I was fortunate to have been part of the technology revolution as a participant in the earliest days of the Internet (DARPANET) and as a pioneer telecommunications engineer, computer engineer, securities analyst, and venture capital investor in many of the technologies now impacting our lives both positively and negatively.

A career in finance and technology gave me the opportunity to attend conferences all over the world, often as keynote speaker. I was constantly approached by attendees wanting to know more about my secrets for lifelong happiness and success. Many people said: "Harry, you should write a book. Tell us about your life and philosophy, and the secrets to your success that have brought you extraordinary happiness, health, energy, and financial prosperity— it would be so inspirational." Fifty years ago, William Exton, a management guru, said to me, "Never say you are going to write a book—just write the book." So, without further procrastination, I did!

The great authors of self-help books written sixty to seventy-five years ago were Dale Carnegie, Dr. Norman Vincent Peale, and Napoleon Hill. They presented strong messages about getting along well with people, engaging in positive thinking, and achieving personal success. When I read their books as a young man, it helped me to focus my mind on being successful and content. This book offers a more contemporary viewpoint that will inspire readers to be happier, healthier, smarter, and more prosperous. There are many books that promote the theme of happiness, but to my mind, in a modern world you also need to be healthier, smarter, and more prosperous. Your chances of being happy will rise dramatically if you pay attention to your health, enhance your education, get a better job, and manage your money appropriately.

We live in a world that is changing more rapidly than ever, necessitating a new approach to achieving success and happiness. Facebook, Instagram, Google, YouTube, Twitter, LinkedIn, and social media in general, have had a major impact in our lives. So has the earlier development of television, computers, mobile phones, and air travel. Change causes stress, so we have to learn to adapt and transform change into a positive rather than a negative force in our lives.

I consider myself to be very lucky. I have been happy all my life even though I started out as poor as a child could be. I lost my father before the age of one. My mother was an illiterate Russian immigrant who could not even sign her name. My three brothers, Sol, Bill, and Bob, who were seven to fourteen years older than me, traveled out of town to find work when they were only twelve to fourteen years old, lying about their age to obtain jobs. At the beginning of WWII they enlisted in the Navy, Merchant Marines, and Marines, respectively. I enlisted in the Army during the Korean War.

My mother cleaned houses because she refused to go on welfare. The rent for our third floor walk-up apartment rose from twelve to eighteen dollars a month through the 1930s and 1940s. Despite living in poverty in East New York, now called Brownsville, that was notoriously known as the "murder capital of New York," I was happy. A Spaldeen (an orange-colored rubber ball) cost only two cents and I played street ball all the time. Yes, a two-cent ball was pretty much all it took to make me happy.

I never had a birthday party or received presents. Life was like that for many during the Great Depression of the 1930s. Why was I happy both then and now? In retrospect, I attribute it to positive thinking and focusing exclusively on happy rather than negative thoughts, and on finding solutions rather than dwelling on problems. I learned that by concentrating on helping others there was little time left for worrying about my problems.

I never believed in "keeping up with the Joneses." I have been married to the same wonderful woman for over fifty years and we have lived in the same house for over forty years. This past year I finally traded in my seven-year-old car for a lease on a new car. I have learned that material things do not provide happiness, but that the proper frame of mind does.

Even though my mother was uneducated she made me go to school every day. Like most mothers she wanted me to be an engineer or a doctor. By age six, I walked by myself to PS 174 in Brooklyn through heavy rain, snowstorms, and high heat. That simple routine helped me develop the dedicated work ethic that I have continued to this day. I have never missed a day of school, work, or sports activities, and have been fortunate to have never been sick a day in my life except for an occasional mild cold. I have never had a headache, the flu, chickenpox, or even a fever, and have never taken vitamins or used drugs or other medications. I must be doing something right.

The wonderful American cartoonist Charles M. Schulz (1922-2000) had a cartoon character who said: "My life has no purpose, no direction, no aim, no meaning, and yet I am happy. I cannot figure it out. What am I doing right?" Unlike this character, I have an idea of what I'm doing and how this can make people happy.

I have flown to China for business over one hundred times and have never suffered from jet lag. Often I fly to Beijing, Shanghai, or Hong Kong and continue on to a remote city in China. I sleep little on the planes, attend a banquet in my honor upon arrival, and return home all within a day or two. Then after a good night's sleep I pitch a double header in a local softball league.

Last year, as the oldest player in the league, I was delighted to be the winning pitcher in the championship game against teams whose players were less than half my age. My success in business and athletics can be attributed to hard work, continuing education, and good genes. My attitude about life contributes to my well-being and could be the most important thing going for me. That is why I am sharing my insights with you.

As for being prosperous, it did not come easily. While working more than fifty hours a week, I was able to earn a bachelor's degree in physics at Brooklyn College and later an MBA with credits toward a PhD in finance from New York University. I then attended a six-month, eight-hours-a-day, special telecommunications program at the Cornell School of Electrical Engineering. All of this was completed in the shortest time allowed by the schools I attended, and involved taking the maximum number of credits each semester and double sessions during the summer.

As Confucius said, "If you enjoy what you do, you will never work a day in your life." I fully agree. I have always enjoyed my work and have been grateful to my employers and colleagues. Of course, a good education, whether it is received in high school, college, or vocational school, can help one make a good living.

However, many workers with little or no advanced education can be successful as well. The lack of a formal education has not prevented courageous entrepreneurs from starting their own business when opportunities for employment were not available to them. The United States is filled with stories of immigrants who have come to our shores with dreams of building a better life for themselves and their families. Through hard work they built successful companies that in the aggregate employ millions of workers. This is what has made the United States great—and the United States is still the best "land of opportunity" in the world.

As far as being smart, it certainly helps to have a high IQ, but even some highly intelligent individuals lack street smarts. People who grow up in poor neighborhoods learn to be street smart by necessity in order to survive. Opportunity knocks for both the underprivileged and the privileged, but often only the street-smart people hear the knock. Family is a great support for most people, but for those without a close and supportive family, there are mentors that include local religious leaders, social services, sports coaches, and friends. Everyone needs a role model to help guide them to success and happiness.

Positivity

Part 1

BE HAPPIER

*"There is only one way to happiness;
and that is to cease worrying about things which are
beyond the power of our will."*—EPICTETUS

*"Happiness is the meaning and the purpose of life,
the whole aim and end of human existence."*—ARISTOTLE

*"Most folks are about as happy as they
make up their minds to be."*—ABRAHAM LINCOLN

Epiphany

When friends, family, and even strangers complain and seem unhappy about the littlest things, I ask myself why. Why aren't they happy nearly all the time? An answer could be that they do not have an attitude of wanting to bring happiness to themselves by spreading happiness to others.

Why not be a comedian or a magician, tell jokes, and do magic tricks to make everyone happy. This was my epiphany when I was young. It's better to be happy than grouchy, better to amuse one's self and others and to participate in events than to just be an onlooker. The world would be a better place if everyone was happy, starting with you.

Chapter One

How to Be Happy

OVER 2,500 YEARS AGO Confucius said, "Life is really simple, but we insist on making it complicated." If only Confucius knew how complicated life would become by the 21st century. Advances in technology and social interaction have grown geometrically and far beyond what anyone imagined just twenty-five years ago, much less 2,500 years ago.

Agrarian economies have been transformed into industrial economies. Local economies have morphed into national economies and then into international economies. The world is changing rapidly on an almost daily basis. Only fifty years ago farmers owned their land and in bad times could at least feed their families. Now, investments, derivatives, and futures have come into being, putting farmers at risk of losing their farms and the ability to live off the land. Machines and robots have replaced human laborers and have created corporate goliaths that ship products anywhere in the world. Great financial fortunes were made, and in many cases lost to competitors, who used newer machines, improved distribution, and modern marketing techniques.

As the world became more complex, the ability to have spontaneous happiness gave way to additional stress and anxiety about the future. With the shift to democratic values and opportunities for all social classes, people could dream of having a better job and obtaining riches of all kinds. This gave rise to hope, but also led to uncertainty and despair. These days, millionaires and even billionaires are crowned, seemingly overnight, when their companies like Uber and Airbnb go public. We are in danger of forgetting that periodically markets crash, causing great wealth to be lost in a matter of hours. The cover story of *Fortune*, February 1, 2015, reports "At Least 80 Tech Startups are Worth $1 Billion or More. Is This Boom for Real?"

In today's extremely complex world where every bad thing that happens is immediately reported, it is more challenging than ever to maintain emotional well-being. But no matter how difficult things may seem, it is actually possible for almost everyone to be satisfied and content, even those considered less fortunate in life, for the feeling of joy comes from within. As Johann Von Goethe said, "Even the lowliest, provided he is whole, can be happy and in his own way, perfect."

The American Industrial Revolution that followed the Civil War and the social media revolution of the 2000s have something in common: they were not foreseen by many. Technology sprouts much like a seed that grows into an oak tree. With every technological advance, life becomes more complicated.

Simpler times made a permanent state of contentment easier to achieve, but the advancement in technology is also a double-edged sword. While technology generally makes people more satisfied with their lives, it can also cause unhappiness. The majority of people benefit from major advances in technology, but there are certainly downsides. For instance, car and air travel can cause accidents and death, traveling can mean going through Transportation Security Administration (TSA) lines at airports, and social media causes great anguish for some.

Inventors working in garages or small home laboratories have changed the world in unforeseen ways despite doubters. Even the most knowledgeable leaders cannot foresee the future clearly as far as what progress humans will achieve.

In 1895 Lord Kelvin, President of the Royal Society, was quoted as saying, "Heavier than air flying machines are impossible." Nevertheless, transportation has progressed from walking to horses, bicycles, railroads, automobiles, and airplanes.

A Western Union internal memo in 1876 stated, "This telephone has too many shortcomings to be seriously considered as a means of communication. The device is inherently of no value to us." Nevertheless, telecommunications has evolved from smoke signals to telegraph, telephone, networks, satellites, and mobile phones.

An executive of David Sarnoff Associates wrote of the radio: "The wireless music box has no imaginable commercial value. Who would pay for a message sent to nobody in particular?" Nevertheless, broadcasting has progressed from radio to television, cable TV, and satellite, transmitted first to homes and eventually to portable handheld devices.

Thomas Watson, Chairman of IBM said in 1943: "I think there is a world market for maybe five computers." Nevertheless, the computer industry has transformed from the abacus to personal calculators, mainframe computers, minicomputers, personal computers, iPhones, and iPads. Unwieldy heavy devices became portable and easy to carry, in much the same way as clocks became watches.

World population has expanded rapidly to more than seven billion people, causing tremendous strains for governments with the necessity of a fecundity of regulation, oversight, and taxation, as well as changes in lifestyles. The European Industrial Revolution of the eighteenth century was but a first step in the development of modern technologies.

Eventually, manufacturing gave way to outsourcing and to services. One-room school houses disappeared and were replaced by large public schools and massive cathedrals of learning at universities. Weaponry developed from clubs, spears, and slingshots to the manufacture of knives, guns, and airplanes, and then to nuclear bombs and cyber warfare.

By the start of the new millennium, humans began texting and talking while walking and even while driving. Children became glued to their portable devices in school, at the dinner table, and in restaurants, disturbing teachers and parents alike.

The average person is often overwhelmed by many aspects of technological progress. The TSA conducts x-rays and pat downs at airports, even for children and the elderly. The National Security Agency (NSA) was found to be downloading information on everyone's telephone calls and emails, causing concern to many law-abiding citizens. Evidently the government prefers to find a needle in a haystack rather than a needle in a thimble of hay.

For the most part, social media like Facebook make people happy, as evidenced by the more than one billion who have become members. But a good number of careers and reputations have also been ruined by entries on Facebook. Internet services such as Google, eBay, and Twitter also have the downside of the possibility for self-inflicted wounds, not to mention wounds by others.

Media technology has also changed our habits. Television coverage of sporting events and the advent of instant replay are making fans less inclined to attend games in person. With added advertising, and the expanded use of replays, games are longer. Moreover, transportation has become problematical and couches are more comfortable than stadium seats, especially in the winter.

The challenge for everyone is to find happiness despite the many obstacles created by technology. Social media delivered through computers and personal devices has revolutionized the daily activities of children and adults all over the world. Who knew that many human beings have an inherent urge to disclose everything they do. They post pictures of themselves (selfies) at work, at play and at parties. They chat with their friends throughout the world instantaneously and incessantly, describing their everyday activities supported by snapshots. WeChat and WhatsApp are highly used apps for this function.

Not too many years ago a majority of people kept to themselves and led lives not of quiet desperation but of happiness. Now I read headlines from *Business Insider*, such as "Seventeen fired for using Facebook" or "Thirteen people got fired for Tweeting." Hundreds of people, especially children, have used apps to bully fellow students, several of whom have committed suicide. A multitude of people have been disgraced or embarrassed by social media. So in the twenty-first century my advice is to take advantage of social media but to do it with utmost care. One thoughtless picture posted on social media could ruin your reputation, career, and even your life.

Idiotic thieves have posted their crimes and shown their loot on YouTube only to be arrested by watchful police. If you have the impulse to tell and show all, you will eventually suffer consequences, either mentally or even physically. Everyone knows that the US government has been intercepting the telephone calls and emails of ordinary people. Did you know that ordinary people are hiring hackers to get into the emails of enemies, friends, and lovers? Just assume that nothing on the Internet is safe from prying eyes.

In the interest of your safety and well-being I will briefly describe the seven leading social media companies and the perils associated with each. There are approximately one hundred social media platforms with more than one million active users. The seven most popular are the following:

Facebook–over one billion four hundred million users.
It seems as if everyone in the world has a Facebook page to keep in touch with friends and family. The downside of this is that Facebook entries have sometimes cost people their jobs, or their prospective jobs, while others have injured their reputations. Robberies have been committed at the homes of people who announce their vacations for all to see.

YouTube–over one billion users.
It is a popular site for video postings. Displays videos made by amateurs, professionals, and advertisers. Billions of YouTube videos are watched daily. Videos range from how to fold a shirt to daredevil acts. Some videos are even cleverly doctored and untrue. People are encouraged to post videos by payment of one to five dollars per thousand views. Need I warn you that videos of you or your family that are embarrassing can come back to haunt you.

LinkedIn–over three hundred million users.
This site is excellent for companies and executives to post job offerings and resumes, respectively. Not much danger here but do you want everyone to see your resume, even your current employer? In 2012 a fast growing app called SlideShare was acquired by LinkedIn. The site offers presentations, documents, and videos. Corporate security is a potential problem.

Twitter–over three hundred million users.
The members of Twitter make comments on topics or personalities in messages (tweets) that are one hundred forty characters or less addressed to specific members for all to see. Instant polling is now the norm for events happening anywhere in the world. Twitter is

a very useful app, but some people have endured criticism of their tweets, and under duress, chose to remove them.

Instagram—over three hundred million users.
This is a photo sharing app favored by women over men two to one. Restrictions are imposed against suggestive photos that are violent, nude, or sexual in content. Children under thirteen are not permitted on the site. Many celebrities post photos on Instagram. Be careful about posting photos that you may later regret having posted. Facebook acquired this site in 2012.

Pinterest—over one hundred million users.
The majority of its users are young females. The site is used by businesses for advertising, and by individuals to display their interests and hobbies. It is popular for displaying scrapbooks about activities or interests. Postings are easily connected with Facebook. There is an option to privatize any or all of your postings. There is not much danger in using Pinterest except for the usual warning about unflattering pictures.

Snapchat—over one hundred million users.
The idea behind Snapchat is that submitted photos are deleted in fifteen seconds. The site is heavily used by youngsters in their teens and early twenties. As expected, several people have figured out how to make the images permanent by taking pictures of them within fifteen seconds. Bullies have used Snapchat to terrorize their targets in the assumption that their messages will permanently disappear in fifteen seconds. Unfortunately for the bullies, the targets have learned to photograph the bullying messages and turn them over to the police. Snapchat also offers businesses the ability to post

advertisements in videos or photos that can last up to a minute. There's not much danger in using Snapchat except for the usual warning about unflattering pictures that may not disappear in fifteen seconds.

Happiness comes from within, so we must not let external forces create unhappiness. As Abraham Lincoln said, "Most folks are about as happy as they make up their minds to be." Happiness is a state of mind, but what exactly is a mind? It is not a physical thing that is found in the human body. For thousands of years philosophers such as Buddha, Plato, and Descartes, and later the father of psychoanalysis, Sigmund Freud, and currently our contemporary great thinkers, have attempted to define this ethereal thing called the mind, which in religious dogma is sometimes equated to the soul. The mind emanates from the brain, but no one knows exactly how.

The brain is made up of approximately thirty billion neurons mysteriously connected by synapses to each other through protoplasmic fibers called axons. The brain physically controls the many organs of the body. Somehow the extensive circuitry of the brain casts off something we call the mind. It is the mind, not the brain, which creates thoughts, feelings, emotions, and memories.

Humans have different IQs, a measurable fact, but a person with a high IQ may have a weak mind, one that is even evil or sick, while a person with a low IQ may have a uniquely wonderful or strong mind. A state of well-being and contentment comes from the mind, not the brain, and fortunately humans have the ability to control their minds. The challenge for all of us is to generate a permanently happy frame of mind.

If the most brilliant thinkers since the beginning of time have offered different definitions of the mind, who am I to add to the great wisdom of the ages? Instead, I offer a simple analogy. The mind is to the brain of a human as fragrance is to a flower. Like the brain, a flower is a complex organism consisting of stamens, pistils, whorls, and stalks. Flowers yield pollen, seeds, and egg cells for reproduction. Flowers can also produce beautiful fragrances, which cannot be seen but are enjoyed by bees, ants, butterflies, and humans.

Send a dozen roses to a loved one and the exhilarating fragrance is likely to bring fond thoughts of the sender to mind. In the same manner, a person in the right frame of mind can exude a pervasive aura that makes other people happy. Flowers range from undesirable dandelions to exotic orchids; there is a wide choice of fragrance.

Following this analogy, consider those who think only of themselves, and think of others who care deeply about family, friends, and even strangers because of a difference in their minds. It is also the characteristics of the mind that make some people work hard and others not. It is the mind that makes people creative, artistic, or athletic. If you want to be happy, it is all in your mind. So take control of your senses, determine to be happy, and develop a frame of mind that will make you and all those around you happy. It is within your control. Positivity is an important element in achieving happiness.

Chapter Two

Young, Poor, and Happy

I GREW UP IN BROOKLYN during the Depression years of the 1930s. It was a hard time for everyone, and that certainly included my family. Technology was nascent. There were few cars in the neighborhood. No one had a television and hardly anyone had a telephone. Airline travel was still a novelty.

Interference from the government was limited, and politics was mostly national. Media meant newspapers since radio was barely emerging, and TV broadcasts were only in the minds of Philo Farnsworth and Charles Jenkins. It was a hard time, but in some ways life was simpler and less stressful as long as people had a home and there was food on the table.

I was born in the East New York section of Brooklyn on the border of Brownsville, the last of four sons separated by more than a dozen years from my two oldest brothers and seven years from my youngest brother. All were born in the 1920s before the Depression changed everything for many Americans. Money was always hard to come by in our family.

My three brothers left home in their early teens to earn ten dollars a week at best. Sol, my oldest brother, lied about his age and moved to Oregon to work for the Civilian Conservation Corps.

Later he joined the Navy to serve in WWII. My next oldest brother Bill also lied about his age and joined the Merchant Marines. He was a gunner in the famous Liberty Ship Convoy to Murmansk that aided the Russian war effort. A majority of the seamen in the convoy died in deadly attacks by German U-boats, but fortunately Bill survived. Bob, my youngest brother, sold magazines in places as far away from New York as Hartford, Connecticut, which in those days was about eight hours by bus from Brooklyn. He too lied about his age to join the United States Marines, surviving WWII campaigns in Saipan and Okinawa.

While still in grammar school, I was the only one left to stay with my mother during WWII. My mother hung an 8 × 12 inch banner with three blue stars (representing her three sons in the armed forces) in a window for all to see. Thankfully, none of the blue stars turned into gold stars representing those who lost their lives.

Both of my parents were born on farms located near Minsk, Russia. They immigrated separately to the United States in 1913 and 1914 just before the start of WWI. Mother became a cleaning woman to make enough money for us to survive. Since I was an infant when I lost my father, I did not have the opportunity to know him. My mother kept in touch with one or two people from Russia, but I never met any relatives, if there were any.

We lived in a third-floor walkup on Hinsdale Street, Brooklyn in a line of twelve identical buildings mirrored by those across the street. The one block on Hinsdale Street between Dumont Avenue and Livonia Avenue was my neighborhood. Virtually all my friends lived on this block that housed approximately one thousand immigrants.

But thinking back to my youth, I remember being happy every day. It may have been partly due to genetics, but I strongly believe that it was also due to positive thinking, a sound philosophy even then—and playing all kinds of sports every day.

I was a good athlete, well known in my neighborhood for that attribute. I played all of the typical street sports, including punchball, stickball, baseball, basketball, hockey, kick-the-can and even football.

A baseball was a sphere of taped-over string, which at one time was the core of a real baseball that had lost its cover years earlier. A typical bat had been broken in at least two parts, but was taped together by electrical tape to resemble a real bat. A football was made of a tabloid newspaper such as the *Daily News* or *Daily Mirror* folded three times and tied with string to resemble the size of a real football. Hockey was played in the street by using the square end of a cheese box as a puck and a goal net drawn in chalk.

Those were interesting times. There were very few cars. I remember one that was parked on a dead-end street where we played punchball. We asked the owner if he would move his car so we could play ball. He came out of his small factory with an iron crank that he stuck in the front of the car and rotated to start the engine, eventually moving the car thirty feet from third base, which was drawn with chalk on the street.

A manhole cover in the middle of the street was second base. Sometimes a bunch of us would just push a car out of the way. Cars had rumble seats in the back where a trunk would be in today's car. They also had running boards that kids would love to stand on while the car was moving.

Not one of my friends' parents owned a car. No one on my block of twenty-four multi-family apartment buildings owned a car. In fact, none of my friends could even afford a bicycle—but we could rent one for twenty cents an hour or one dollar a day. However, many of my friends did have roller skates.

The still very dangerous and poverty-stricken neighborhoods of East New York and Brownsville were known back then as the "murder capital of New York." Recently the *New York Times* called it one of the poorest neighborhoods in New York. Things haven't changed much in seventy years. The population consisted of mainly Jewish immigrants who were poor, working-class families. But Jewish and Italian gangsters lived in the neighborhood, and it was notorious as the birthplace of Murder, Inc., the American Mafia formed in the 1930s and 1940s.

The gangsters wore expensive overcoats and were highly respected by the neighbors. Poor people are sometimes driven to do bad things out of desperation. Things were so bad that a few neighbors on both sides of our street committed suicide by jumping off the roofs of their four-story buildings.

Instead of going to the beach (an hour by subway for five cents) we took blankets to the roof, which we called "tar beach," to get some sun. One day while we were on the roof my next-door neighbor's dog Mitzi ran after a bird and leaped off the roof to her death.

I did not even know any of my neighbors unless they had children my age. In Brooklyn you kept to yourself. There were few, if any, community activities or organizations. We could not afford the twenty-five cents a week it cost to have me attend the nearby Yeshiva for religious education.

Starting at the age of four, I read the *Daily Mirror,* which cost two cents a copy and when folded and tied with rope occasionally served as a football. I read the comics and sports sections. Just about everyone in Brooklyn was a Brooklyn Dodger baseball fan except for a small minority who declared themselves Yankee or Giant fans just to provoke us Dodger fans. Professional football, hockey, and basketball existed in New York but were outside the neighborhood focus of most Brooklyn residents.

We never saw football, basketball, or hockey games because there was no TV, and when I was a small child there was also little radio coverage. But later, radio announcers would keep us glued to our sets as they read a telegraph description of a baseball game, making up things as the game progressed and banging a stick on a wooden block to simulate the sound of a bat striking the ball. We were mesmerized. Life was simple and fun.

Every day we would get together after school to play ball in the streets or in a school playground. Occasionally an old lady would scream at us to stop making so much noise. We had no adult supervision or coaches. Teams were formed by choosing captains who selected players alternately. Players were chosen when a captain threw a bat in the air, which was caught one-handed by the other captain. Each captain gripped the bat above the other's grip until there was no room left at the top. The top hand won, but there was a catch: if you could get your fingertips on the top of the bat and swing it around your head three times, you received the first pick.

We also played games like "ring-a-levio," in which two teams were formed and one team had to find members of the other team in hiding and tag them to be placed in jail until all rivals were caught. A similar game was hide-and-seek. We played hide-and-seek, but I did not know the name of the game until I grew up, I always thought the name was "hingoseek." We played "Johnny-on-the-Pony" where one kid would bend at the waist with arms outstretched and his hands against a wall. His teammates would line up one after another behind him in a crouched position holding the waist of the boy in front of him. An opposing team of boys would then jump one at a time on the line hoping to make them fall down on the sidewalk. The idea was to jump as high as possible with legs spread and to come down hard on the backs of the kids on the opposing team. Aiming for a weak, skinny kid was often a winning strategy.

We did not think about being poor. This was our life and we enjoyed it. All the kids in the neighborhood seemed happy even though I do not remember ever going to a birthday party. Movies were five cents and later ten cents to see a double feature plus a cowboy serial which always ended with the featured cowboy, such as Tom Mix or Roy Rogers, in great peril. On Fridays the movie theater would even give out a small prize such as a dish.

The Police Athletic League (PAL) distributed tickets for New York Rovers hockey games. The Rovers were a farm team of the New York Rangers, and some of the players even graduated to play for the New York Rangers. More importantly, the PAL also distributed tickets for Brooklyn Dodger games—the biggest prize of all! Sometimes we went to a Dodger game by saving box tops or deposit bottles. (Yes, there were deposits on milk bottles in those days.)

I never bought food at Ebbets Field because I could not afford a pretzel or a hotdog. Instead, my friends and I would bring lunch in a paper bag. Lunch was a sandwich consisting of peanut butter and jelly, bologna, or salami and a treat such as a Devil Dog or Twinkie. There were no night games. Of course we sat in the bleachers. Grandstand seats were one dollar and way out of our reach, but were something to aspire to. We walked three miles to reach Ebbets Field. Sometimes we would spy a player from the Dodgers walking to Ebbets Field and would walk alongside, happily chatting. That was a thrill! Many of the Dodger players had nicknames like PeeWee Reese, Pistol Pete Reiser, Cookie Lavagetto, and Shotgun Furillo.

All of my friends had nicknames too; one of my best friends was called Squeezie. He once squeezed his older sister's breast and was spanked by his father. When his father reprimanded him, Squeezie is reported to have said "it was werf it." Another friend, Charlie Garland, or "Jolly," was held in high regard by everyone because he claimed he was related to the most famous movie actress of the time, Judy Garland. It was not until many years later that I learned that the real name of Judy Garland was Frances Ethel Gumm. Jolly Garland's ruse was not exposed until many years after we had grown up. I lost track of Jolly Garland, but he probably moved on to a successful political career. Ironically I was called "baldy" because of the large crop of hair on my head.

Later I was nicknamed "Happy Harry" because of my disposition. Nicknames were well-earned and sometimes the opposite of a distinguishing characteristic or physical feature. The few kids who could afford eyeglasses were all called "four eyes." One of my friends was called "Foxy" because he was not too bright. At the age of eight he said he could outrun an automobile, so Foxy and a gang of us waited on the street for a car to approach. At last a Plymouth came into view. We stood about thirty feet behind Foxy, and when the Plymouth reached Foxy he ran as fast as he could alongside. Down Hinsdale Street Foxy and the Plymouth sped along, side by side. Livonia Avenue was fast approaching. (Remember that in those days directional signals were not yet invented.) Upon reaching Livonia Avenue, the Plymouth made a left turn. Unfortunately, Foxy running with all his might ran straight ahead into the Plymouth.

A bottle of Pepsi Cola cost two cents at the neighborhood candy store called Cheap Phil's. I think I was raised on Pepsi Cola rather than milk. I loved the bubbly sensation in my throat. My favorite toy was a five-inch square block of wood with a spinner nailed to the middle. Lines were etched from the center to the edges forming triangles. Inside the triangles were inscriptions such as 1B for single, HR for home run, FO for fly out, GO for groundout, etc.

My friends and I would play this "baseball" game for hours with that simple toy made by one of my older brothers in a shop class ten years earlier. We kept score on a piece of paper and dramatized our make-believe game using a lineup of Brooklyn Dodger players versus the hated opposition. These days, children may still be more interested in simple toys such as playing with a cardboard box rather than the expensive game or toy that was in the box. Wealthy parents tinged with guilt feel compelled to ignore this fact.

Another game we played was watching an occasional car go by and using the last digit of the license plate to represent an out or a hit, with a six representing a single, seven a double, eight a triple and nine the Holy Grail—a home run. We would spend hours sitting on the curb waiting for enough cars to go by to complete a nine-inning game. The inning-by-inning line score was scrawled in chalk on the street, which we called the gutter.

Home telephones were just coming into use, but there were telephone booths in some candy stores. We did not have a home telephone until my teens when we finally had a party line installed, which meant sharing the line with a neighbor. If you picked up the telephone and heard someone on the line you had better hang up or the other party would scream at you. The candy store on my block fortunately had a telephone booth. On the rare occasion when one of my brothers called, someone would yell up to my third floor window calling for my mother or me. One of us ran downstairs as fast as we could because someone was paying a lot of money per minute for a long-distance call. We thought that only rich people could afford long-distance calls.

To avoid using a two cent-stamp we would walk two miles to pay our monthly electric bill at the electric company office on Pitkin Avenue. We never bothered to calculate the value of the wear and tear on our shoe leather.

My upbringing in the Depression years of the 1930s and the economic recovery years of the 1940s demonstrates that poverty does not preclude happiness. My family and friends lived in hard times, but were generally happy. A poor person can be made happy by the slightest spark of good fortune, such as a victory by their favorite team, a visit to a park or museum, playing a game, or just talking with friends. A rich person may require more expensive things to make them happy, such as dinner at a favorite restaurant, smoking an expensive cigar or owning a car.

Some people who have achieved a certain level of wealth are hard pressed to maintain their happiness when setbacks occur. In this regard, the poor who learn to be happy by the simpler things of life such as family, friends, and books may have an advantage over wealthy people who can more readily lose what they have. The lesson is that perpetual happiness comes from within. So develop a mindset of positivity.

Take courses at night school; enroll at a vocational school or college. Prepare a resume, a different one for every job that you seek. Fill your life with hope and dreams of the future while being satisfied with what you have.

After I served in the United States Army during the Korean War and went to college on the G.I. Bill, I held numerous jobs and was happy in all of them.

After graduating from Brooklyn Technical High School I got my first real job. I earned forty-four dollars a week as a draftsman for a telephone switchboard company. On the first day of work I wore a white suit that belonged to my oldest brother who was two inches taller. It had very wide lapels and looked like a Zoot Suit. It was a cold day so I put on a green coat with protruding fibers that was owned by my second oldest brother. The suit pants dragged way below my ankles and the jacket was too long. I looked a mess, but fortunately no one laughed when I arrived at the office for my first day of work. They knew I was trying my best.

My next job was at the Brooklyn Navy Yard as an electrical designer and eventually an electrical engineer. From there I enlisted in the Army at the time of the Korean War. After an honorable discharge I reclaimed my job at the Navy Yard and attended Brooklyn College in the evenings taking the maximum number of credits allowed by the school including double summer sessions. All of this was paid for under the GI bill. I was in a hurry to get a proper education and improved employment. Sixteen-hour-days in school and work were the norm for me.

I graduated from Brooklyn College with a Bachelor of Science degree in physics, and then attended the New York University Graduate School of Business where I received an MBA and started a PhD program, but did not complete it. Meanwhile, I worked full time for AT&T and the New York Telephone Company. AT&T added to my education at the Cooperstown Data Training Program, a three month, forty-hour per week school. In addition, I was sent to a six-month advanced training class in telecommunications at the Cornell University Graduate School of Electrical Engineering.

I left AT&T to work in the nascent Internet industry that was called DARPANET. I was Vice President of Sales and Marketing for the two leading data terminal companies serving the Internet industry. From there I joined the largest computer company in the world. No, it was not IBM, but Sperry Rand Univac headed by General Douglas McArthur. Armed with a background in telecommunications and computers I went to Wall Street, eventually working for three major investment-banking firms. I was the first securities analyst to cover both computers and telecommunications. It was not long before I was one of the most quoted people on Wall Street. That led to many consulting opportunities with large and up-and-coming companies in the telecom, computer, and software fields. I gave keynote speeches at virtually all of the major technology forums. My speeches were given without notes or slides, a practice I have continued to this day.

I left Wall Street and formed Edelson Technology to consult and advise corporations. The CEOs of two of the world's largest multinational corporations, Charlie Brown of AT&T and Martin Davis of Gulf + Western (now Viacom), asked me to be their advisor and consultant. They also asked me to invest some of their corporate funds in venture capital sectors that might be of interest to their companies. Over the years, eight other multinational corporations joined with AT&T and Viacom, including Asea Brown Bovari, Colgate Palmolive, Cincinnati Bell, 3M, Ford Motor, UPS, Reed Elsevier and Imation. Edelson Technology invested in well over one hundred technology companies throughout the world and achieved a superb 27 percent internal rate of return (IRR) without the benefit of leverage (borrowing).

Throughout college and in my business endeavors I have analyzed situations and focused on solutions. I have followed the solutions orientation in many of the articles I have written on topics such as philanthropy, technology, investments, venture capital, and boards of directors. Often the articles led to positive actions by both corporations and philanthropies. In the numerous speaking engagements I have made throughout the United States, Europe, and Asia, I have endeavored to be creative and provocative using the Socratic method of teaching (asking questions rather than just lecturing).

I have had the pleasure of meeting some of the most successful business people in the world including Steve Jobs, Bill Gates, George Soros, Wilbur Ross, and Ross Perot. They were all driven to succeed and were extremely happy pursuing their lofty goals. I read dozens of business plans every week prepared by entrepreneurs who wanted to emulate the highly successful legends who preceded them. The entrepreneurs and management teams behind these businesses are all driven to succeed. Many do, but others fail—and try again. The path to success is laden with failure. Look at drug discovery. Researchers may fail in their experiments a thousand times before discovering a new drug.

Success is measureable. A baseball player is considered excellent if he has a batting average of 300, a success rate of three out of ten. An entrepreneur only has to succeed once to be considered a success. A venture capitalist may have only one or two winning investments out of ten or twenty and can still be considered successful. Regardless of being successful in business, remember the ultimate goal in life is to be happy, not to be wealthy. There are numerous ways to be happy, including the joy of spending time with family members and soulmates or pursuing an interest in music, sports, cooking, reading, and many other hobbies.

Chapter Three

Old and Happy

From the beginning of civilization, philosophers have opined about happiness. Before social media, before newspapers, even before books, early philosophers gained recognition through word of mouth. Eventually these thoughts were written down and fortunately survived through the ages.

The earliest known philosophers may have been in the Vedic age in India, as far back as 2000 BC. Confucianism and Taoism flourished in China around 500 BC. Greek and Roman thought came later and today is taught in most Western universities. Most college graduates know about the Greek philosopher, Socrates, whose teaching style was to ask his students questions to pull ideas from them rather than just lecture. And what was his reward? Socrates was tried by the State for treason and found guilty. He was sentenced to death and died from hemlock poisoning.

Socrates was a teacher of Plato who in turn was a teacher of Aristotle. In a like manner, every religion has passed on the teachings of their earlier philosophers and virtually every philosopher has written about happiness. However, do the teachings of the great philosophers of the ages make you content and fulfilled today? I think not. What makes you happy is something that is happening to you now, whether it is through entertainment, someone you recently met, receiving a promotion, the favorable outcome of a sporting event, nice experiences with your family, or pleasant daily occurrences. The goal of this book is to provide contemporary ways that will make you happier, healthier, smarter, and more prosperous. Learn from the past, but live and learn in the present!

IBM was one of the companies I followed closely when working as a securities analyst on Wall Street. Japanese computer companies were threatening IBM's dominance, so in the 1970s I visited the chairmen of companies like Fujitsu, Matsushita, and Nippon Electric. On each visit, before our conversation started, the chairman would bring forth a series of pages describing the company's philosophy and values. I was impressed that the success of each company was built on a philosophic foundation. In college I studied Greco-Roman philosophy as well as a smattering of philosophies and religions from other cultures, including Indian, Judaic, and Christian.

Later, business dealings brought me to China. I visited the mountain where Taoism began and learned about Confucianism and Buddhism. I am not a scholar of these religions and philosophies, but have learned something which has sharpened my own experiences. I have developed a personal philosophy of life that has made me happy throughout every day of my existence. It can be summarized as: "Strive to be happy, work hard, help other people, and focus on solutions rather than problems."

One essay that has contributed to my thinking was written in 44 BC by Marcus Tillius Cicero, the famous Roman philosopher and orator. The essay, "De Senectute," describes the benefits of growing old as opposed to the doubts and concerns brought on by old age, senility, and fear of death.

Back then, old age was thought to begin at the age of forty-five. Cicero wrote his essay on aging, an absolute masterpiece of logic and persuasion, when he was sixty-two. A year later he was accused of treason, found guilty and sentenced to death. Cicero was beheaded and his hands cut off because his hands symbolized the power of his writings, which still resonate today.

Cicero's narrative on old age is through the voice of Cato the Elder, a learned man who died at age eighty-four a hundred years earlier. Cato advises two eager and curious young men, Scipio and Laelius, and Cicero pens a famous dialogue among the three men.

The reason the essay appeals to me, and I hope to you, is because Cicero deftly turns every posited negative conjecture into a positive. The young men are told that there are four reasons why old age can lead to unhappiness: (1) withdrawal from daily activities; (2) the body grows weaker; (3) the deprivation of physical pleasures; and (4) old age brings one closer to death. Upon reading the essay we learn an important lesson—to think positively rather than negatively. Personally, I do this every day of my life to good effect. When you have time, read this thirty-nine-page essay, which is available on the Internet.

The first reason for unhappiness in old age, withdrawal from daily activities, is dismissed by describing the exploits of elderly generals, famed politicians, and legendary poets. Cicero gives an example that the elderly captain of a ship may merely hold the tiller instead of working at the pumps or climbing the masts, but what he is doing is more important than what the young, relatively inexperienced crew is doing. The second reason, that growing older makes the body weaker, is dismissed with the thought that there are always men who are stronger than others, but this is of no consequence because a man needs only the strength to do what he must do. As to the charge that old age impairs the memory, Cicero avers that this depends on the person. He provides examples; e.g., Themistocles has such a strong memory that he knew the name of every citizen in the commonwealth.

The third reason, that growing older disqualifies one from the enjoyment of sensual gratifications, Cicero determines that it is a positive. To no longer require sensual pleasure means "that old age delivers us from those snares which allure youth into some of the worse vices to which that age is addicted." Sophocles, when he became old, was asked if he engaged in amorous commerce with the fair sex. "Heaven forbid!" replied the venerable bard, "... and glad I am to have made my escape from the tyranny of so imperious a passion."

To the fourth reason, that being old means being closer to death, Cicero responds that young people are more exposed to mortal accidents than the aged, and that old people are already in possession of that length of life which young people can only hope to attain. When people complain about the aches, pains and grievances of growing older, Cicero puts them down by stating "... complaints of this kind, relies in the man, not the age." After all, young men also complain.

As a sample here are a few excerpts from "De Senectute":[1]

> SCIPIO: I have frequently, Cato, joined with our friend Lae-
> lius, in admiring that consummate wisdom and virtue, which
> upon all occasions so eminently distinguishes your charac-
> ter; but particularly, in that singular ease and cheerfulness
> with which you seem to bear up under those years which
> are pressing upon you. I could never observe that they are
> attended with the least inconvenience to you: whereas the
> generality of men, at your time of life, usually complain of
> old age as the heaviest and most insupportable of burdens.

CATO: . . . Now it cannot be supposed that nature, after having wisely distributed to all the preceding periods of life their peculiar and proper enjoyments, should have neglected, like an indolent poet, the last act of the human drama, and left it destitute of suitable advantages. Nevertheless, it was impossible but that in the life of man, as in the fruits of the earth, there should be a certain point of maturity, beyond which the marks of decay must necessarily appear: and to this unavoidable condition of his present being, every wise and good man will submit with a contented and cheerful acquiescence. For to entertain desires repugnant to the universal law of our existence; what is it, my friends, but to wage war, like the impious giants, with the gods themselves?

SCIPIO: Yes, my venerable friend; like travelers who mean to take the same long journey you have gone before us, we should be glad (if it be not imposing too much trouble upon you) that you would give us some account of the advanced stage at which you are now arrived.

CATO: . . . I particularly remember to have often heard Caius Salinator and Spurius Albinus (men of consular rank and nearly of the same age as myself) bewail their condition. The principal subject of their complaint was, in the first place, that they were no longer capable of enjoying the sensual gratifications without which, in their estimation, life was of no value; and in the next, that they found themselves neglected by those who had formerly paid their court to them with the greatest attention. But they imputed their grievances, I think, to a wrong cause. For had they arisen merely from the circumstance of their age, they would have been common to myself, and to every other man of the same advanced years. But the fact is much otherwise; and I have known many, at that period of life, who passed their time without the least repining—who neither regretted that they were released from the dominion of their passions, nor had reason to think themselves treated with disrespect by any of their connections. In fact, the true grievance, in all complaints of this kind, lies in the man and not in the age. They whose desires are properly regulated, and who have nothing morose or petulant in their temper and manners, will find old age, to say the least of it, is a state very easily to be endured, whereas unsubdued passions and a forward disposition will equally embitter every season of human life.

I am writing this book at an advanced age, but while I may not be as limber in mind and body as I used to be, according to my friends and doctors I am in the upper 10 percent of people in the mastery of activities that I pursue.

For example, I pitched our team to victory in the finals of the local Softball League. In the playoffs, I pitched a doubleheader beating the number three and number one teams and then our team beat the number two team for the championship. Except for my son, who is in his forties, the rest of our team is in their mid-twenties, which can lead to Saturday night activities that can cause them to be a little under the weather for Sunday morning games. Although I am by far the oldest player in the league, I have never missed a game for illness since the start of the league in 1974. However, I did miss three games when my wrist was broken by a batted ball, so I coached instead of playing for that period of time.

I am as active in business today as I have ever been, working six days a week assisting companies on numerous transactions. In order to process all the reports and proposals I receive, I sometimes read at my maximum speed of 4,000 words a minute. There is no backlog in my life because I read everything the day it is received.

I can memorize one hundred things given to me in any order and recite it back in any order in fifteen minutes. I do math in my head, which in college helped me shout out answers faster than others using calculators or slide rules. Because I have mental curiosity, I have learned math tricks that I relate in later sections of this book.

I recently took courses in both Mandarin and word processing. I also gave six extemporaneous speeches at the United Nations, the Harvard Club, Cornell University, Columbia University, NYU, and a Life Sciences Summit. When necessary, I read a book in an evening. When I speed read a legal brief and place notes in the margin, I always ask my partner, who is a lawyer, if I missed anything, and he always says no.

Getting old does not necessitate becoming lazy and unhappy with nothing to do. Growing "old mentally" is a mistake! At home, I still rake my leaves, mow my lawn, and shovel snow. Do not make an excuse that you are too old. Just do it, and you will be surprised how easy some of these tasks are and how good they make you feel. My desire is that everyone who reads this book will be as happy and smart as they can possibly be.

Chapter Four

Focus on Solutions
Rather Than Problems

EVERYONE SEEKS HAPPINESS; some achieve it all the time, some part of the time, and some always seem to be unhappy. Early in the history of civilization, happiness was a favorite topic of philosophers and religious leaders. Even today, libraries are filled with books on how to achieve self-fulfillment and joy, which is an indication of how hard it is to achieve. Why is that so? The reality is that feeling content with one's lot is a state of mind, and everyone is capable of attaining it with the right mental attitude.

Surprisingly it is easy to eliminate negative thinking just by focusing on positive images, events, or ideas. Imagine standing in front of a full-length mirror. The mind of the person looking back at you from the mirror is your foe. You will win the battle because you can punch the mirror and smash it to smithereens, but it cannot punch back. You can control your behavior, but your image cannot.

At a conference twenty years ago a young lady approached me who was decidedly miserable and contemplating suicide. I asked her why, and she told me that her misery and sadness came from several events in her recent past. Her parents divorced and her boyfriend of three years left her. She was employed but had little in savings.

I asked her if there was anything good in her life, anything that made her happy. For five minutes she related the positive things in her life. Her new job was working out well, and there was the possibility of a promotion. Her mother, whom she was very close to, was in good health, and the breakup in her marriage could be looked upon as a positive event because it had not been working out for over five years.

The young lady said that her health was very good, and she enjoyed hiking, skiing, and tennis. I suggested that she focus on the positives in her life and not the negatives. When you are feeling sad the trick is to focus on what is good instead of what is bad, and on solutions rather than problems. I suggested that she make a list of her problems and next to each problem list one or more solutions. She asked for my business card and sent me a heartfelt letter telling me that because of our discussion she was happier than she had been in years.

I am not a man of the cloth like Dr. Norman Vincent Peale, but it does not prevent me from spreading happiness to others. Everywhere I go, whether it is checking into a hotel, going to a security desk at an office building in Manhattan, talking to the garage attendant or to a secretary, I make a friendly remark, compliment people on their clothes or their looks, and everyone smiles back and is uplifted.

When I check into a hotel I ask if an upgrade is available for the Presidential Suite; when checking in at the security desk at an office building I ask if the picture on my driver's license looks like Tom Cruise. When I talk to the elevator operator in a large building I suggest that no one will get anywhere without his services. When I talk to the office receptionist, I ask why they hide a person so lovely in a remote office. Everyone seems to enjoy the banter and has a good laugh.

In giving a speech, which is generally monthly, I always start with a humorous remark or short joke that is pertinent to the group and the particular venue. As a result, in the first minute of the presentation, the entire audience is alert, looking directly at me and smiling. I have the audience in my grasp, so even if I stutter or stammer, no one will notice. I sprinkle a few pertinent jokes throughout the speech and usually end the speech with one as well. There are thousands of jokes and humorous anecdotes, and I can always recall appropriate ones for the occasion. Old jokes can easily be recycled and modified to fit in with current events and personalities.

Whenever attendees are asked to fill out an appraisal of the speakers, I am always rated at the top. Why? Because I make people think and feel involved. I do not use PowerPoint presentations because I want everyone looking at me and not a screen. I do not use notes since I have studied mnemonics and can easily remember the five, six, or ten key points that I wish to make without losing a bond with the audience.

Not everyone can be happy all the time. There are bad marriages, drug addicts, alcoholics, penniless people, unattractive people, poor sports, single people who have not found soulmates, losers in politics and sports, and on. While most people cannot feel upbeat and positive all of the time, they can become much more content with life by focusing on solutions to their problems and asking for counsel from friends or family. People love to be asked for their advice. It makes them feel good about themselves if they can help someone else. In his poem "The Rainy Day," the poet Henry Wadsworth Longfellow wrote "Into each life some rain must fall." But also remember the saying "April showers bring May flowers." Turn the negative into a positive.

Feeling good and joyful about life does not come easily, but I have found that the harder you work, the luckier you seem to be.

When I was getting an education I always felt that when I completed high school or college, the accomplishment would be permanent and would be on my resume the rest of my life. The same is true of employment; every job is a learning experience and an enhancement to a resume.

Feel good about yourself. If you lose a tennis match or a golf game, it is nothing to brood about—just focus on improving your game. If you have a child whose team fails to win a baseball championship game, remember that more can be learned from losing than winning.

As they say, "Sometimes a black eye makes you see more clearly." Many athletes take losing too seriously. What they should think is, "If I got two hits today instead of going hitless we could have won the baseball game. I should practice more to become a better player." Parents can get coaches for their children to improve performance, in sports or in their studies.

Isn't it funny that the harder people work the luckier they seem to be? Hard work normally pays off. If it does not or if your effort is not properly recognized it may be time to seek other employment. Young people joining the workforce often take almost any job available because they need the money and do not have the experience or credentials to get the job they really want. There is always time to earn those credentials.

I spoke to a twenty-eight-year-old young man who could not afford to get a college degree when he was younger. He was thinking of going to college in the evening, but it would take him five years to obtain a degree. This seemed like a long time to him. I reminded him that he would be thirty-three-years-old five years from then whether he went to college or not. Patience is rewarded.

Chapter Five

Achieving Permanent Happiness

How can the amorphous term "happiness" be defined? Is it a transient experience, or can it be a permanent part of our being? A street beggar can be made very delighted by receiving a five-dollar tip. An athlete can be equally ecstatic if his football team wins a game or even wins the Super Bowl. In general, human beings are joyful when they marry, graduate, obtain a job, or get promoted. People can be happy one moment and sad the next.

This book is not geared to a discussion about transient moods of happiness. It is about learning to be content with one's self and life in general all the time—morning, noon and night—every day of the year. Happiness is a state of mind and can be achieved by anyone if they set a goal to achieve it. There is no bar to achieving happiness. Whether poor or rich, ugly or beautiful, physically handicapped or athletic, employed or unemployed, soldiers in battle or couch potatoes, partisan Republicans, Democrats, or Independents, you can be happy almost all the time.

Setbacks in life such as losing a game, job, or election need not make one unhappy except for the moment. People who think positively welcome the challenge to recover from personal setbacks.

Challenges should be considered exciting and must be engaged in enthusiastically. People who suffer defeats, experience great tragedies, or are seriously challenged, have to pull themselves together and relish the opportunity to recover by winning the next game or election, by obtaining a new job, or by moving on gracefully to the next phase of their lives.

I do not want to belittle the many problems people face. It could take a great deal of time to recover from misfortune. The idea is to try your best to overcome misfortune and get on a positive track with the help of family and friends. Take heart from people less fortunate than you who have shown remarkable courage and fortitude. Many war veterans, who have been physically and mentally impaired by their experiences, have learned to function well through the help of veteran organizations and family support. In the same manner, children who are physically challenged experience joy by participating in the Special Olympics. There are ways to get out of the doldrums by participating in what life has to offer.

Naturally, it may be harder to be happy if one is mentally disturbed, refuses to work, drops out of school at an early age, repeatedly curses his or her plight in life, beats a spouse, or neglects one's children. Regardless of who you are and your station in life, you can change your life for the better and be happier every day. I will reveal to you the secret of accomplishing this goal.

If happiness comes from a certain state of mind, you must develop that state of mind. The power is within you. The first step is to think positively. Limit your complaints about the minor inconveniences of everyday life. Do not complain about your spouse or partner, your lack of a spouse/partner, your children, job, boss, political representatives, or favorite teams. Instead of complaining, take appropriate action and feel better about yourself.

The Brooklyn Dodger baseball team habitually had bad seasons, but the favorite expression of Brooklynites was "Wait Till Next Year!" What a great expression! It brought joy instead of depression to the denizens of Brooklyn. That kind of thinking is a start. There is always the potential of a brighter future.

Some people are so troubled by their present situation that they cannot think straight. I knew an executive who had bounced around Wall Street and finally landed a high-level position at a medium-sized investment bank. He worked at this bank for nine and a half years.

One day he called to tell me that even though he would earn a pension of one million dollars if he remained employed only six more months, he could not stand working there a day longer and was going to quit the next week. He was a good friend of mine, so I offered some simple advice—endure! Find a new project that will benefit your organization. Get energized about a new facet of your activities. Do not do anything rash. Lie low in the weeds and be productive for the next six months. Afterwards, every time I saw him he would say "I am being productive in new ways and I am lying in the weeds."

Needless to say, he not only stayed six months, but for eighteen months, and earned a handsome pension. Sometimes peoples' judgments are clouded by stress, illness, or other serious concerns. I believe people frequently approach me for advice because my mind is clear, and I am always eager to help. I have trained myself to think positively and focus on solutions rather than problems.

The smartest, richest, handsomest, and most beautiful people are just as likely to be unhappy as those who have opposite traits. Improving one's life through marriage, education, or learning street smarts can help people achieve happiness more readily. Nevertheless, no matter how high a position one achieves in life, and no matter how rich, educated, or good-looking one is, you may still be unsatisfied and feel depressed and low unless a proper frame of mind is developed.

Work on it. Think positively about everything. Wipe every negative thought from your mind. Make the best of every occurrence. If you are a student and get a B on a test, so what! You are still going to get a passing grade. Dwell on the positives. On the next test you may get an A; all you have to do is study more. Put grades in perspective. Once you find a job, no one will be concerned about your grades. The only thing that will count is your performance.

Personal catastrophes are unavoidable. Deaths, accidents, bad economic times, and divorce are inevitable obstacles on the road to happiness. You must learn to overcome such obstacles regardless of how serious they seem at the time. I just established a new friendship with a well-known economist. His wife passed away twelve years ago, and he was in mourning for all that time until he met a wonderful woman who is now his girlfriend. His thinking changed from despair to having a joyful attitude. My advice to him was, "Marry this woman and get rid of your lingering despair."

People have to recover from unfortunate circumstances much more quickly than this economist. Do not linger on the negative occurrences in your life. Move on.

Chapter Six

Being Happy Every Day

IF YOU WANT TO INCREASE your pleasure in living, or help others find theirs, here are some suggestions. First, determine to be content and upbeat. It is as simple as that! Happiness comes from within, although external factors can play a role. You must win the battle within your mind. You have the ultimate power to be happy by looking at everything in a positive rather than a negative way. I have been happy throughout my life through thick and thin, success and defeat, and accomplishment and failure because I created a mindset to be happy that was made easier by a foundation of hard work and a good education. However, anyone can become consistently happy by winning the battle to develop a positive mindset.

Today, as every day, I got out of bed eager to read the newspaper and go to work and accomplish things. It snowed overnight so the first thing I did was shovel my driveway. It always feels good to accomplish something, even if it is only shoveling snow or raking leaves. Moreover, when I start a job I always finish it and that makes me feel good. Every day should be full of small and large achievements, which can include chores, preparing meals, or helping children with homework or sports activities—a myriad of small things that are taken for granted, but are actually accomplishments.

There are daily achievements and there are long-term accomplishments, such as graduation, marriage, and attaining higher-level employment. All activities big and small contribute to make life fulfilling.

Take heart from the fact that almost every person with a serious disease or injury has a strong will to live, even in a diminished lifestyle. War veterans may return from battle with severe mental or physical impairments, but frequently they and their families carry on because just being alive is wonderful. Parents with children who are autistic or have other serious infirmities love their children and often will not give up on them for anything. Happiness can come to all regardless of circumstances. No matter what the obstacles are, remember that things could always be worse. So think positively.

To be happy does not mean you cannot become angry about something. It could be that your anger may be warranted, and it may even be good to get it off your chest. But anger should be harnessed to make a point and achieve a goal—not used to upset yourself and make excuses for your behavior for an extended period of time.

When people direct anger and blame at you, it is often caused by something else that is going on in their lives, so do not overreact to this. If you have a family member, roommate, tenant, or friend who bugs you no end, do not allow it to be a perpetual thorn in your side. Do something about the problem or stop complaining. It does not pay to harbor anger.

What can you do? Talk to the offending party or have an intermediary do it for you. Take legal action, if necessary, as a last resort. The point is, do not let anger linger. If a friend is a constant irritant to you, get a new friend. If you have a problem at work with your boss, talk with your boss, ask for a transfer, or seek new employment through friends, an employment agency, or the Internet. You could also learn a new trade at night school, intern for a tradesman (plumber, mechanic, carpenter), or become a salesperson (such as for Mary Kay, Avon, or a car dealer). Just do not be a constant complainer; instead learn to remediate problems. If you are a sports fan and your team stinks, but prices for seats keep rising, you can stop attending the games to send ownership the message: "Improve the team or I will settle for watching games on TV."

In undemocratic foreign countries or in countries with rigged elections, the only answer for people may be to riot in the streets in an effort to bring down the regime. In free countries like the United States, there are elections that can change representation at local and national levels. Citizens who fail to vote should not complain about who is in charge. If you are unhappy with the way your municipality or the federal government is run, you have the option of participating in the election process by voting, contributing money to the candidates of your choice, or volunteering your services. The mantra is: do not complain, do something. Just the process of doing something will make you happier.

Positive thinking is a must for those who want to be happy. For example, at the first sign of a possible illness, many people will say, "I am coming down with something." Those people are usually correct because they talked themselves into being sick. When I have a sniffle I always say, "It is nothing; I am not coming down with anything." I have always been correct. People who get sick despite a positive attitude need to use medicine (cold medicine, sore throat lozenges, etc.) and if their condition is more serious, make a visit to the doctor.

There have been numerous scientific studies showing that people can be talked into healthy or unhealthy states. For example, in trials for new drugs, subjects may be divided into three groups: those receiving placebos (usually harmless "sugar pills"), those who are receiving the existing drug, and those receiving the new drug. Time after time a large number of those receiving the placebo have nearly the same beneficial effects as those receiving the real drug.

A nocebo is when a patient is given a harmless sugar pill and told that it may have harmful side effects such as dizziness or nausea. Many patients drop out of trials because they experience those side effects even though they were only taking sugar pills. The mind is the key factor here, and it is under your control. There is undeniable scientific evidence that positive thinking works.

The famous Hawthorne effect came from an experiment at a Western Electric factory. Workers were told that the company was improving the factory environment by introducing better lighting and air conditioning. Afterward, productivity rose even though no improvements were made. Similar empty promises were made again and again, and productivity always improved. It seems that workers performed better if they thought the company was looking out for them. I once read about two people in a rowboat, one of whom was allergic to bee stings. The man spied a bee in the boat, believed he had been stung, and died from panic. No bee sting was ever found.

If the thought of having too many things to do stresses you to the point that you do nothing, just start doing things one at a time in an organized manner. I organize errands at home by geographic proximity. At the office I organize telephone calls by time zone. A series of in-person meetings in New York City are organized by location. Written matter sent to me is read immediately if responses are required, or more leisurely later in the day if time is not of the essence. Good organization leads to efficiency and the saving of time.

There are many ways of dealing with stress. I was the first to arrive at a dinner party for eight, when the six-year-old daughter of the host couple spilled grape juice on the dining room rug just before the other guests arrived. It was a simple problem that had several solutions. The hostess could make an attempt to clean the rug herself, apologize to her guests about the stain, or rant and rave at the child and ruin the dinner for her guests. She chose the third solution and ruined the dinner for all. In reality, the guests are unlikely to care a whit about the stained rug.

Another example of a situation that can cause anxiety is "second guessing" our decision making. If you are driving and approach a fork in the road, and decide to take the left fork, do not complain of taking the wrong fork because you find there is heavy traffic. After all, the fork not taken could have had even heavier traffic. Instead, the solution is to observe your GPS to see if there is an alternative route, and stop complaining because it will not do any good. Why complain about something that is out of your control?

Whenever there is a problem, focus on solutions A, B, and C and not on the problem. After all, the problem has already occurred, and there is nothing you can do to prevent it. If your spouse crashes a car, do not yell and nag; just call a tow service and extricate yourself from the predicament. Yelling and nagging will only aggravate the problem and prolong the agony.

Education always helps one to be happy. It is not necessarily the certificate or degree that is important; it is the knowledge and confidence that is gained. Education comes from reading books, taking night school courses and Internet programs, or engaging in a traditional education in grade school, high school, and college. Education is more obtainable than ever because of the Internet. Information found on Wikipedia and through a Google search can answer almost any question. A set of thirty encyclopedia books is no longer the sign of an educated family. A little pocket device can hold access to more information than even a million books. There is no excuse for failing to expand your education.

Finding or getting a job brings happiness. Children may enjoy opening a lemonade stand, mowing a neighbor's lawn, shoveling snow, or delivering newspapers because they like the idea of making money and being useful. Warren Buffett, one of the richest people in the world, started out by delivering newspapers. He developed a work ethic and learned that he enjoyed making money.

Modern technology can greatly help to enhance our work lives. Websites like ZipRecruiter, Beyond, LinkedIn, and Monster can aid in the search for a new job. It is not easy to switch jobs during poor economic times, but there are always possibilities. I took a job in the computer industry at half my salary because I recognized that it would open the door to more opportunities. It was not long before I topped my previous salary.

People could do what I did, for example: they could work at a tailor shop or with a mechanic on the weekend, for very little or no wages, in order to learn a new trade. If you want to be a couch potato and not work as hard as you can, you reduce the chances of being happy, and statistics indicate you will probably die earlier than normal. Most immigrants work two or three jobs to improve their lot in life.

The savings rate in other countries is much higher than in the United States. Here we like to spend money even before we make it—thanks to credit cards. Get in the habit of saving a percentage of your salary every payday. This is easy to accomplish if your employer has a retirement plan such as a 401k, especially if it matches your contributions. Having a bank account, certificate of deposit, or a stock investment is necessary for a rainy day, but it also provides peace of mind.

Family relationships provide a firm foundation for maintaining happiness. It is important to maintain those family relationships. Communicate in person, by telephone, email, or social media. Not everyone has stable family relationships because of divorces, squabbles, and a host of other things. Whether or not you have a close family relationship, it is helpful to join a group such as a book club, sports team, community center, veteran's organizations, church group, and so forth. Firemen provide a good example of having a strong bond. They eat, sleep, play, and fight fires together; they depend heavily upon one another.

Hobbies are fun, whether they are mostly physical, as in skiing, aerobics, or tennis, or using your hands in carpentry, knitting, and making jewelry; and they often require extensive knowledge, especially when collecting things like coins, stamps, or antique cars. Many people with hobbies end up making their hobby a full-time occupation.

Hobbies provide peace of mind because people really enjoy them. It is always good to be an expert at something, and for most people it is their hobby that is their specialty. Competitive sports are a great outlet for enjoyment, either as spectators or participants. If you do not have a hobby, get one—whether it is dancing, creating things with your hands, cooking, gardening, or collecting. If you want to add to your skills, take courses in the day or evening.

Planning for the future encompasses decisions about education, employment, marriage, children, where to live, and family matters. If you are young, you may want to take special courses that will better prepare you for college or a particular career. If you are a young adult, you will want to meet like-minded people by joining organizations and having friends with similar interests. If you are married, planning will involve children and whether or not you should eventually move to a house in the suburbs or an apartment in a city. If you are older, you may contemplate moving to a state with warmer weather, cheaper housing, or lower inheritance taxes. Everyone should have a plan for the future.

Here are key points to finding happiness:

- ▷ Win the battle of the mind; determine to be happy

- ▷ Spread happiness wherever you go

- ▷ Use positive thinking (positivity)

- ▷ Focus on solutions, not problems

- ▷ Educate yourself

- ▷ Develop a hobby for you and your children

- ▷ Join local clubs; get involved

- ▷ Seek healthy entertainment

- ▷ Expand friendships

- ▷ Lead an active life

- ▷ Be thankful for what you have

If you do even half of the suggestions above, you will be a happier person. If you are doing these things you are probably already enjoying a life you find fulfilling.

Part 2

BE HEALTHIER

"Health is a state of complete physical, mental and social well-being, and not merely the absence of disease or infirmity."—WORLD HEALTH ORGANIZATION

"If you keep saying things are going to be bad, you have a chance of being a prophet."—ISAAC B. SINGER

"To keep the body in good health is a duty ... otherwise we shall not be able to keep our minds strong and clear."—BUDDHA

Epiphany

Why spend a half hour packing gym bags and going to a gym when you can exercise in your normal activities by walking upstairs or taking a long walk?

Why not walk several miles a day between consecutive meetings in the city? Why not go to work by walking a mile to the train station and a mile at the other end of the trip instead of driving a car to the parking lot and taking a taxi or public transportation at the other end of the trip?

Chapter Seven

The Secret to Being Healthy Is Being Happy

PART 1 OF THIS BOOK is about being happy; Part 2 is about being healthy. The sequence makes sense because there is general agreement by health professionals that happy people are the healthiest people. Study after study has shown this to be a fact. Well-known pediatric surgeon and author, Dr. Bernie Siegel, is quoted as saying "The simple truth is that happy people generally do not get sick." I am the embodiment of that thought since I am always happy and have never been sick.

Quite simply, the main reason for my good fortune is positive thinking, since I am neither an exercise addict nor a health food devotee. Genes play an important role, but to the extent that you can control or affect your health, positive thinking is the answer. Optimism is at the heart of positive thinking.

When I hear friends and relatives say, "I think I am coming down with something," I always argue against that statement by offering words of encouragement, such as just telling them: "You are not coming down with anything." When you are tired and feel weakened, you are susceptible to negative thoughts that just may allow illness to prevail. When I cough or sneeze and people suggest that I am coming down with something, I always say: "It is nothing; I am fine." The illness that other people suggest never materializes.

A positive mindset is an absolute must for being happy and healthy. Miserable people are more likely to be in poor health. Good health is not about engaging in mysticism, but rather about increasing your chances of having good health. Disease can strike anyone at any time, but if it occurs, a proper positive frame of mind can diminish the consequences. Any doctor will tell you that this is true.

Let me tell you about my funny experiences with the medical profession. When in first grade my teacher escorted me to a small office to meet with two ladies. I did not know the purpose of the meeting, but soon enough two huge earmuffs were placed over my ears. The earmuffs would now be called earphones of ancient vintage. One lady instructed me to raise my right hand every time I heard a beep. I never raised my hand. The ladies began talking about me. The first lady said to the second lady, "He is deaf, completely deaf."

Now I was only six years old and I thought I knew the definition of "deaf," but thought maybe I was ill-informed. I could clearly hear the ladies talking about me so I thought perhaps being deaf meant not as good at hearing as other people. The ladies summoned someone else to come into the office who I now think was a nurse. The nurse said, "First you have to plug the machine in," and left the room. I proceeded to hear a series of humming noises and was escorted back to my class.

About ten years ago I had a physical exam by an internist. Everything was fine, but he sent me to a cardio specialist in the same building. The cardiologist had me run on a treadmill for approximately ten minutes. I ran at higher and higher speeds while telling jokes and having a great time with the nurses. Afterwards the cardio specialist told me I had a blockage. I said, "Really?" That's pretty surprising because I play tennis and baseball and have never had a problem with my wind or heart. I asked how serious was the blockage? He said 70 percent.

I asked what he suggested. The doctor said I needed an angiogram. I laughed about it, but secretly was interested in taking another test that would show what good shape I was in. At the hospital after undergoing the test I awakened from the anesthesia and shouted out to the doctor, "How did the test turn out?" He replied: "I would trade my arteries for yours any day." Subsequently the insurance company refused to pay the doctor, saying that there was no reason to give me an angiogram.

On another occasion I had a checkup conducted by an urologist. A few days later I sat across the desk from the urologist who had a very stern expression on his face. I cheerfully said, "What's up doc?" He said the lab report on my urine sample indicated a severe urinary problem because my chromosome 32 was not right and neither was chromosome 65. I really don't remember the chromosome numbers but that was the gist of it.

I said, "You must be kidding. I have no trouble with my bladder or kidneys; everything is in fine working order. You must have someone else's lab results." I demanded a new test. The results came back that I was perfectly normal. The urologist was not quite convinced said, "Let's redo the test." The third test came back normal.

What do my experiences illustrate? If you get a bad diagnosis, it certainly helps to get a second opinion. Not the kind that Rodney Dangerfield joked about. He went to a psychiatrist and was told that he was crazy. Rodney demanded a second opinion, and the doctor said, "OK, you are ugly too." I mean get a second opinion from a doctor of even higher authority than the first doctor. There is a widely quoted number of twelve million people annually being given a wrong diagnosis. The overall figure may be wrong, but the problem of missed diagnoses, otherwise known as false positives, is a real problem. So think positively, even when given a negative diagnosis.

The healthcare and information technology industries are undergoing profound changes that will make people healthier and able to live longer. Many new therapeutic options are emerging because of advances in molecular medicine that are creating vaccines and drugs that mitigate or heal serious illnesses.

The 1962 discovery of the double helix structure of the human genome has led to breakthrough science in fields as diverse as chemistry, nanotechnology, and bioinformatics, which are converging with information technology to enable the development of novel personalized applications for patient treatment. The highly promising use of genetics to diagnose and treat both healthy and sick individuals is covered in chapter 11.

Doctor visits will be enhanced by breakthrough research in wireless life sciences, which will enable patients to be monitored from afar by medical specialists. Breakthroughs include ingestible miniature sensors that will allow doctors to determine if patients are receiving the proper dosage of medication as directed by their genomic profiles.

Significant progress is being made that will allow physicians using mobile devices to access electronic medical records, X-Rays, and MRI scans. Lightweight wearable devices equipped with cellular modems and GPS chips will give physicians the ability to monitor patients in real time after they leave hospitals. The convergence of genomics and information technologies will provide unprecedented improvements in personalized healthcare to optimize disease prevention and treatment.

The Human Genome Project has made available sequences of the slightly more than 20,000 genes that make up the human genome to accelerate understanding of the biochemical abnormalities that underlie human illness. This knowledge has generated many new molecular targets for treating disease. Driven by advances in proteomics, immunology, customized medicine, drug delivery, and other areas of emerging research, new therapeutic options will increase sharply as conventional medicine evolves into personalized molecular medicine. Breakthrough science in information technology and nanotechnology are rapidly being adapted to healthcare applications. In short, new technologies and services are profoundly changing healthcare in diagnostics, treatment, and the way it is delivered.

If you can manage to live a little bit longer you may be able to survive a great deal longer because of critical advances in medical technology. So if you are ill, hang in there. Advances in diagnostics ranging from single drop blood tests to genetic testing are helping to identify diseases and inherited traits earlier than ever before. Treatments of pernicious diseases such as diabetes and cancer have improved to the point where they have been totally eliminated in some patients.

Longer life expectancies have revealed a serious and expensive problem, namely Alzheimer's disease. Decades ago, when life expectancies were shorter, many people died that would have been stricken with Alzheimer's disease if they had lived longer. Now Alzheimer's is a scourge of the elderly. The Alzheimer's Association estimates that the 2014 costs of Alzheimer's was $214 billion, $150 billion of which is paid for by Medicare and Medicaid. Nearly two-thirds (3.2 million) of those with Alzheimer's disease in the United States are women. In fact, women in their 60s are two times more likely to develop Alzheimer's disease in their lives than they are to develop breast cancer. Sixty percent of caregivers of Alzheimer's victims are unpaid women.

This disease can strike anyone at any age, including the rich, the poor, the powerful, and the powerless. The Alzheimer's Association opines that if you are 85 or older, the chances of getting Alzheimer's disease if you are white is 30.2 percent; if you are black the number is 58.6 percent, and if you are Hispanic, 62.9 percent.

The most well-known person to have Alzheimer's was former President Reagan. The billions of dollars going into the research of Alzheimer's disease, to determine the cause and how it can be alleviated, is bearing fruit. Several methods of early detection of Alzheimer's disease have been announced but are not yet in wide use. One promising method is simply to examine the eye.

What are individuals to do in this new era of healthcare technology? It all comes down to fundamentals, as is the case for basketball, baseball, and soccer teams. Sports teams that are well versed in fundamentals will often beat competing teams possessing greater talent. The fundamentals of good health are a sound diet, adequate exercise, optimism, positive thinking, and excellent medical care that include regular checkups. Notice that I did not include the indiscriminate use of vitamins and unregulated health supplements. Several studies have cast doubt about their effectiveness, and many have cited the possibility of dangerous side effects.

Chapter Eight

Think Your Illness Away

Let the Placebo Effect Work for You

YOU KNOW HOW IT IS when a child says to her mother before going to school for a test, "I have a stomachache," and the mother replies, "It is all in your mind." Well, mother is probably right. The brain is a physical thing that sits in the top of your head, while the mind is ethereal, loosely connected to the brain in a complex and mysterious manner.

Humans are born with brains that have measurable IQs, but there is no measurement for the mind because it is not a physical thing, and its workings are largely unknown to modern science. As I have stated, the mind can be compared to the soul, hard to define and hard to understand. But the mind is a wondrous thing, for better or worse. The mind generates thoughts that can make you happy or sad, healthy or sick. It can develop genius, stupidity, evil, or benevolence. The mind can make someone spiritual or an atheist, a Democrat or Republican.

Isn't it wonderful that so powerful a force as the mind can be controlled by you? As I have maintained here, I control my mind to the extent that I am always happy, healthy, and industrious with a positive attitude about life. What is your mindset?

On the negative side, our mind creates superstitions, and most superstitions are unhealthy to have. Few would disagree with the fact that almost all things regarded as superstitions are stupid. The origins of most beliefs regarded as superstitions date back to ancient times and are attributed to occurrences that members of the nobility thought would bring bad luck into their lives. This led to the great majority of people believing for no logical reason that certain behaviors and events would bring bad luck. Superstitions are just passed on from generation to generation and have become a part of our culture.

Superstition is defined as an irrational belief in the consequences that will occur from violating specific everyday activities. These consequences will be delivered by evil spirits or other unknown forces. How ridiculous is that. Do not believe in superstitions that give you a negative mindset. By definition, superstitions stem from irrational beliefs.

If you have to believe in superstitions, believe in positive ones. For example, King George II was riding in a carriage when one of the horses acted up. A nearby chimney sweep grabbed the horse and saved the king from possible serious injury, whereupon King George II issued a royal decree that chimney sweeps are bearers of good luck. King George II is someone to be admired for that act. Doesn't every sovereign want their subjects to think happy thoughts?

When I hear people say a black cat crossing their path is bad luck, I immediately think that seeing a squirrel is good luck, or better yet, seeing a bird is great luck. After all, there are more birds than squirrels and more squirrels than black cats. I only believe in good luck, not bad luck. I would rather be in a happy frame of mind than be upset.

All day long I see examples of good luck. If I wake up at 6:06 I think *pair of sixes—that is good luck!* If I look at the clock and it is 7:11, I think *that is really good luck.* When I check my coat I look at the ticket stub, and if it is fifty-two I think *five and two is seven and that is a good luck number.* The Chinese believe that eight is a lucky number, and some would pay a million dollars for a license plate of all eights. Every time I see a wild animal such as a deer or a rabbit I think that is exceedingly good luck. It is no wonder I am happy all the time. Good luck is in the air.

Here are eight of the most popular negative superstitions—all of which are widely believed and practiced. Do not have a bad day because of a stupid superstition, especially if it is Friday the 13th.

1. The number 13 is unlucky

2. Breaking a mirror will bring seven years of bad luck

3. Walking under a ladder will cause misfortune

4. A black cat crossing your path is dangerous

5. Knocking on wood assures continued good fortune

6. Opening an umbrella indoors is bad luck

7. Spilling salt is bad luck unless some of it is tossed over your shoulder

8. A bird flying into your window is a bad omen

The only superstitions that are of concern are those that may ruin your day by creating negative thoughts. Those who believe in superstitions that bring bad luck can improve their lives by creating their own superstitions that bring good luck. If you win a lottery, create a positive superstition by attributing your good fortune to wearing a baseball cap backwards on that day or some other silly thing. The new superstition may live on for hundreds of years, and your name may be associated with it in future history books.

How can you develop a mind that makes you happy, healthy, smart, and prosperous? It is not difficult. People achieve a proper frame of mind in many ways including positive thinking, religious sermons, spiritual books, biographies and learning from parents, friends, and teachers. You may be an old codger, a spoiled brat, a disadvantaged person, a New York Mets, or Chicago Cubs fan, but there is hope for all because control of the mind is entirely up to the individual.

If proof is needed to support the contention that the mind plays a significant role in producing happiness and healthiness, look no further than the concept of placebos and nocebos. The idea that providing positive reinforcement to a child, student, athlete or patient produces positive outcomes has been known for hundreds if not thousands of years, but never been adequately proven until the 1950s.

Theories are a dime a dozen, but in the scientific world of mathematics, physics, and engineering, theories must be proven to be validated. Evidence of what is now known as the placebo effect was hearsay for thousands of years. Now it is a proven fact based on thousands of controlled scientific studies.

Gradually the placebo effect, as it came to be called, was proven time after time in double blind studies of new pharmaceutical drugs. "Double blind" means that patients and doctors did not know which pills patients were given—the "sugar" pill or the real pill. The placebo effect is reminiscent of the development of facsimile machines, which were around for fifty years before they took off and came into the mainstream for use by the general public as the common fax machine.

Now, thousands of studies and articles in medical annals faithfully describe the placebo effect. A stark and trail-blazing example was provided by Henry K. Beecher, a medic treating wounded American soldiers during World War II. He ran out of morphine so what did he do? He told the soldiers he was giving them morphine while actually infusing them with simple saline solutions. Approximately 40 percent of the soldiers reported that the saline solutions eased their pain. In 1955 Beecher published a book called *The Powerful Placebo* that many critics derided. His book created a stir, but ultimately Beecher was proven to be correct by numerous independent controlled studies. The placebo effect was legitimized!

Anecdotal evidence was buttressed by thousands of clinical pharmaceutical trials, but as in many cases of seemingly clear results, there were two sides. On one side is the obvious conclusion that one's health is affected by implanting thoughts in patients. On the other side are the pharmaceutical companies and medical professionals who have much to lose if patients can have improved outcomes by just taking sugar pills and being sweet-talked. While there is no doubt that FDA-approved pills produce healthier outcomes, there is also no doubt that thinking positively is a good way to contribute toward a healthy outcome.

If the following explanation of placebos and nocebos does not convince you of the power of the mind, then nothing will. In Latin the word placebo translates to "I will please;" nocebo translates to "I will harm." Placebos induce healthy or positive outcomes while nocebos do the opposite, inducing unhealthy or negative outcomes. Placebos and nocebos can be harmless pills containing no active ingredients. The difference between a placebo and a nocebo is merely the advice offered to the patient.

A harmless sugar pill, placebo cream, or even sham surgery that is offered to a patient along with positive reinforcement by a researcher or doctor describing the promise of beneficial results, is called a placebo. The same inert pill, placebo cream, or sham surgery, accompanied by advice suggesting the likelihood of unpleasant side effects, is called a nocebo. Approximately one third of patients are made better or worse depending solely on the instructions provided by the doctor or researcher, and thus the term "placebo effect" or "nocebo effect" describes this phenomena.

In a controlled double-blind study, half of the patients would get a new pill that could cure or alleviate a disease, while the other half would get the placebo. Amazingly, in such carefully orchestrated drug trials, anywhere from 20 percent to as high as 80 percent of the patients given the placebo experience very positive results—in some cases, just as positive as the real pill.

In 2013, 173,025 registered clinical trials were conducted throughout the world, 68,870 of which were in the United States. It has become standard procedure to include a placebo as part of a trial. Often, one group in a trial receives no treatment and serves as a control group to observe the normal progression of the disease. The Hippocratic Oath taken by doctors contains language stating that doctors should not harm patients. This practice is a conundrum for doctors because the use of placebos and nocebos is rife with the potential for harm. For example, patients may argue that they should have been given the drug being tested rather than a placebo. Moreover, nocebos actually can cause harm.

There are tens of thousands of examples of the effects on subjects from placebos and nocebos. Here are just a few examples starting with controlled studies and ending with two anecdotal cases. It will give you an idea of the powerful influence of verbal counseling.

▷ A February 2015 edition of the Science Times section of the *New York Times* reported on a study published by *Neurology* in which twelve patients with Parkinson's disease were told that two drugs were being tested. One drug cost $100 and the other cost $1,500 per dose. All twelve received an identical injection of a plain saline solution. The so-called expensive placebo achieved better results than the lower priced one by a ratio of two to one. The benefit of the $1,500 placebo was about the same as that of levodopa, the most effective known medication for Parkinson's disease. The reaction of all the patients ranged from incredulity to astonishment.

▷ A recent study was undertaken to determine if Omega-3 was effective at relieving painful arthralgia in women taking aromatase inhibitors. Two hundred-fifty women were randomized to take either Omega-3 or a placebo for twelve weeks. The researchers were amazed to find that 55 percent of the patients taking the placebo had clinically significant improvement.[2]

▷ Researchers at the Harvard Medical School enrolled eighty patients suffering from irritable bowel syndrome. Half received no treatment, while the other half received pills clearly marked "placebo" and amply described by the doctors as similar to sugar pills. The placebo pills were taken twice daily. At the end of the three-week trial 59 percent of the patients taking placebos reported adequate symptom relief as compared with thirty-five percent for the control group.[3]

▷ The *Washington Post* reported that three medical centers did a study of aspirin and another blood thinner in heart patients. At two of the medical centers, patients were warned about gastrointestinal problems, one of the side effects of aspirin. At the third location, patients were not told about the possible side effects. The result was that those warned about the potential problems were almost three times as likely to have the side effects, even though actual stomach damage such as ulcers was the same for all three groups.[4]

▷ Michael Witthoft did a study with G. James Ruben at Kings College London and published in the *Journal of Psychosomatic Research* in 2013. One hundred forty-seven test subjects were divided into two groups. Group one was shown a BBC documentary that dealt with the potential health hazards associated with cell phone and Wi-Fi signals. The other group watched a report on the security of Internet and cell phone data. Both groups were then exposed to fake Wi-Fi signals that they were told were real. Fifty-four percent of group one reported agitation, anxiety, and tingling in their arms and legs. Two subjects left the study early because their symptoms were so severe they no longer wanted to be exposed to radiation.

▷ A team of Italian gastroenterologists asked people with and without lactose intolerance to take lactose for an experiment on the effects on bowel symptoms. The subjects did not receive lactose, but rather glucose, which does not harm the gut. The result was that 44 percent of the subjects who were lactose intolerant and 26 percent of those without lactose intolerance complained of gastrointestinal symptoms.[5]

▷ Ikemi Koackagowa enrolled thirteen hypersensitive students in an experiment. They were touched on one arm with leaves from a harmless tree, but were told that the leaves were from Japanese trees that produced effects similar to poison ivy.

On the other arm the subjects were touched with poisonous leaves, but the subjects were led to believe were from a harmless tree. All thirteen subjects displayed a skin reaction to the harmless leaves but only two reacted to the poisonous leaves.[6]

▷ Decades ago the Fieschi procedure for treating angina pectoris was the standard. A young cardiologist named Leonard Cobb tested its efficacy. He operated on seventeen patients, eight with standard Fieschi procedure. But on nine of the patients he only made tiny incisions, but did not tie knots on the mammary arteries, which was the way the Fieschi procedure was accomplished. The result was that the sham surgery patients did as well as those who had the Fieschi technique. The experiment ended the use of the Fieschi technique.[7]

▷ In Alabama, Vance Vanders had a problem with a witch doctor who put a foul smelling liquid in front of his face and told him he was going to die. Vanders went home and began to deteriorate. Emaciated and near death, he was taken to a hospital where doctors could find no cause for his symptoms. After a few weeks his wife told one of the doctors (I'll call him Dr. X) about the hex. Dr. X lied to Vanders, saying that he contacted the witch doctor and choked him until he explained how the curse worked. He told Vanders the witch doctor had rubbed lizard eggs into Vanders' stomach, which hatched inside his body and were eating Vanders from the inside out.

After relating this concocted story to Vanders, Dr. X injected Vanders with a solution to make him vomit, which he did uncontrollably. Then Dr. X showed him a green lizard, which he had hidden in his black bag and said, "Look what has come out of you Vance." The next day Mr. Vanders woke alert and ravenous, quickly regained his strength, and was released one week later.[8]

▷ In 1957 a new so-called "wonder drug," Krebiozen, looked like the final solution to cancer. A hospital patient heard of Krebiozen and demanded to take the drug. He did, and had a miraculous recovery as the tumors melted away, returning him to a normal lifestyle. Then the patient happened to read a negative article on Krebiozen, declaring that it did not deliver the promised relief. Immediately the patient had a relapse as his tumors returned.

The doctor tricked the patient by telling him that he would be given an improved version of Krebiozen but was really just distilled water. Once again the patient fully recovered after the placebo treatment. Unfortunately the patient died two months later after a newspaper reported that Krebiozen was totally ineffective.[9]

Encouragement works! Think positively and believe in wellness. Abolish negative and unhealthy thoughts.

Placebos and nocebos prove that our mind is a wonderful thing that can be manipulated for good or bad. If you are smart you will take advantage of the placebo effect every day of your life. Be optimistic rather than pessimistic. Think positively instead of negatively. Spread happiness to the people around you. Do good deeds for others, because not only will it make others happy—it will also make you happier. Wake up every day glad to be alive and raring to go to work, whether your work is at home or away from home.

Complete your chores and bathe in the accomplishments. Cleaning a closet or a room should make you feel good. Raking leaves or shoveling snow are chores that must be done and should make you proud of your efforts. Hard work, whether by a farmer or urbanite, provides feelings of fulfillment and enjoyment. Hard work should become a habit. Your mind is for you to control. The bottom line for every person is to be happy, healthy, and successful. Having contentment should be life's goal and you have the power to make that happen.

Chapter Nine

You Can Conquer Stress

IN THE FILM *Wall Street,* the lead character Gordon Gekko glori-
fied the word "greed," intimating that it was good. In a like manner I would say that stress is good; however, anything in excess
is bad, especially when referring to stress. Stress is a fact of life.
Everyone has stress to one degree or another, whether it's a child
doing show-and-tell in class, an adult working at a difficult job, or
a family undergoing problems. A little bit of stress is a good thing,
it is known to improve performance.

The problem with stress is that it can elevate to a point where
you cannot sleep, when you scream at the slightest provocation,
and when you can't think straight. When you are stressed out you
have to do something about it. Confidence defeats stress; so does
a positive mindset, going on vacation, exercising, and pursuing an
education or a better job. The inability to handle stress often leads
to unhappiness and poor health.

Stress can come from a single event, such as an accident, flood,
fire, or death of a loved one. That kind of stress is unavoidable, and
you just have to cope with it. It is everyday stress that is a problem
that must be solved or alleviated. There is no reason to be stressed
out about ordinary occurrences in life, but it happens anyway.

Some people are stressed out during routine activities with their family, job, or just watching their favorite sports team on TV. Why is it that some people handle stress with aplomb and others fall apart? Are there ways to reduce stress or even eliminate it? The answer is yes, but sometimes the solution requires things to get worse before getting better.

Solutions can include a diversity of things, such as getting a less stressful job, even a divorce, winning the lottery, joining clubs, and making new friends.

Parents are sometimes upset by the actions of their children and vice versa. Make the best of it. Try logic or have discussions with family members to find ways to lessen your stress. If that doesn't work, learn to live with the situation.

Stress is an acceptable response in exceptional circumstances, but perpetually stressed out people need help. They need to adopt new ways of reacting to common stressors. Earlier I mentioned that statistics show healthy people are happy people. It is also true that stressed-out people are unhealthy people.

Everyone knows about stress, but it can still be hard to define. While a little stress may make you perform better, a high level of stress may affect you in highly adverse ways. You may not be able to think straight. You may spend all of your time worrying. Stress can lead to physical symptoms such as elevated blood pressure, dizziness, and loss of sex drive. Stress may make you moody and angry, even depressed. You may lose your appetite and may not be able to sleep well. Many friends and business contacts have come to me with problems they cannot solve because they are stressed out. Often I find solutions to their problems almost instantaneously because I am thinking of solutions while they are mired in thinking about their problems.

One day, a long time ago, I was driving to Maine by myself. In preparation for the trip a local garage rotated the tires on my car. There I was on the Maine Turnpike cruising along at 70 mph when suddenly my car spun 180 degrees and I was facing two terrified drivers who were previously behind me. One of my wheels had come loose and rolled off into the woods.

After the initial shock my training in dealing with severe problems took hold. I gripped the steering wheel tightly and kept the car in the lane as it careened along the highway bumping against the center divider. I guess people would call that a stressful incident, but after the initial shock I did not feel any stress at all as I just tried to make the best of a bad situation in real time.

Soon enough my car came to a stop and the cars following me pulled to the side of the road to see if I needed assistance. One of them called the police and a tow truck. I waited peacefully, feeling no stress as the situation was remedied. Why did I act with utter calm while others might have been severely shaken? The answer could be that it is in my genetic makeup, or it is more likely that my mind has been trained to react to events with calm.

Let's turn to everyday living, rather than once in a lifetime incidents. I play baseball a lot, and have often batted in the last inning of close games and come through in the clutch because that is what good players do. I also own a number of stocks, which go up or down every day. A few investors that I know, who are active in the same stocks, panic whenever the stock price drops sharply. Others like me do not react. After all, stocks go up or down every day, so why react to a normal occurrence. The only reaction that is necessary is to sell, hold, or buy the stock.

Harboring angry feelings does not help the situation one bit. Aside from taking action on the stock, I could call management to find out what happened and then make a decision on buying, selling, or staying put.

People get very upset at election time when the candidate of their choice loses. It could be in a national or local election or even a union or school election. My advice is to either get over the loss or take action—such as by contributing money or providing services to your candidate of choice in preparation for the next election. Do not be a sore loser since this does you no good. If you are in a restaurant and someone at the next table knocks over a candle setting fire to the room, would you get out of the restaurant immediately or would you stay there and berate the guilty party at the risk of your life?

Years ago, one of my friends, a beautiful and talented woman, called me with a plaintive declaration at 10 p.m. on the eve of her wedding. She was going to marry a good-looking, nice guy, a senior executive of a major corporation. A gala reception following the wedding ceremony was scheduled at the Plaza Hotel in New York City the next day. I was aghast to learn that my friend wanted to abandon the wedding at the last minute. She had been divorced once and was getting cold feet. I went over the facts with her. She knew her fiancé quite well, having been engaged for two years. He was a great guy and talented in many ways, including his skill in athletics. She was now in her early forties and unlikely to meet someone else as good as him. Cold feet was not a reason to call off the wedding. She offered no logical reason for her apprehension. I convinced her to proceed with the wedding. She agreed with me. The wedding ceremony was great, as was the reception.

It is now twenty years later. The marriage worked out perfectly. They are still madly in love. We keep in touch, and I am glad to know that there is little stress in her life, and she has wonderful new hobbies that she enjoys immensely. The moral of this story is that stress can lead to bad decisions.

Everybody knows that stress in excess is bad for health. Stress creates anger, often causing fights with yelling and screaming, and bad decisions. People under stress cannot sleep well; their blood pressure and pulse rates rise, breathing becomes difficult, and this can even lead to a heart attack. So why not give thought to figuring out how to deal with stress? Simple situations can be stressful to one person but not another. Why is that so? Counseling from doctors, psychiatrists, clergymen, teachers, family, and friends should be sought out by people who react stressfully to ordinary events.

As an example, someone who owns a house or summer home may undergo stress when the value of the property declines as it commonly does during a recession. There is no reason to suffer stress in this situation unless the property is going to be sold. If you are not going to sell your house or summer home, just ride out the ups and downs in valuation, and do not give it a second thought. The only price that counts is when the house is sold.

Unemployment is a more serious problem that often causes stress. Stress is of no benefit to an unemployed person. Oncoming stress should be diverted by taking action such as obtaining unemployment insurance, creating a new resume, informing friends about your situation, and looking at online services and newspaper want ads. Action is the counterbalance to stress; going into action puts you in charge of the situation.

There are stressful events in our lives such as taking tests, interviewing, giving speeches, or getting married. Preparation, like action, is a countervailing force to stress. There are students that panic before taking important tests. They cannot sleep, they drink alcohol, they party, and they over-study. A good night's sleep is more important than studying too much.

Unhealthy reactions to stress abound. Overeating is a common reaction to stress. At a movie theatre moviegoers munch on giant bags of popcorn during action films. It is when overeating becomes habitual, leading to a serious weight gain, that this response to stress becomes worrisome. Other reactions to stress like biting nails or failing to do a job properly are also unhealthy. I know people who stress out because of concern about the weather in faraway places. A severe storm or tornado somewhere in the United States or in Bangladesh or China will cause worry or concern to many people, even though there is little they can do about it. Is a disaster thousands of miles away sufficient reason to feel stress? I think not.

People worry about far-away relatives they have not seen in years. They carry around a feeling of dread and concern about occurrences happening to almost everyone and everything. Some people live a life of stress caused by things that are entirely out of their control. They worry about family, friends, victims of crimes, poor people, hungry people, war refugees, and dozens of other things. They are empathetic to a fault. They are the best of people in the worst of health.

However, like most people, I limit worrying to my immediate family. If something concerns me or I feel I can do something worthwhile, I contribute my time or money to worthy causes. Worrying about things I cannot fix is not doing me or anyone else any good. Other people, organizations, and politicians are getting paid to take care of those concerns. I do not want to sound merciless, but I believe in Alfred E. Neuman of *MAD* magazine whose motto was "What, me worry?"

Chapter Ten

Being a Couch Potato
Is Not All Bad

YOU DO NOT HAVE TO BE A NUTRITIONIST to know that you are what you eat. Humans require nutritious food and drink to maintain health and vigor in the same way that airplanes, trains, and cars require energy for propulsion and toys require batteries to work. Some fuels and batteries are better than others. It is the same with food that people consume. Theories and advice on diet and exercise abound, but there are no clear-cut rules. Are people who take an assortment of vitamins daily really healthier than those that do not? Do obese people have less energy than thin people?

Every so often studies are announced that defy expectations. Surprising promulgations have been made, such as vitamins are unnecessary and cause more harm than good; people who are a little heavier than normal live longer than others; or marathon runners have higher levels of coronary-artery plaque than a control group of sedentary men.

What are we to believe—the common wisdom or the results of individual studies? Every person is different. The placebo effect and positive thinking play an important role. Those who consume massive numbers of vitamin pills daily, run marathons regularly, or eat the so-called correct foods may benefit from the placebo effect even if their compulsions are off the mark. I may be an outlier, but I do not take any pills, do not exercise in a gym, watch what I eat, but still love to eat hamburgers and pizza occasionally. To my way of thinking, whatever you do is fine as long as your health is good. If a doctor advises you to lose weight or to take vitamins to cure a deficiency, I would take the advice.

We all know obese people who are full of energy and thin people who lack energy. Energy is only one aspect of health. There may be serious side effects of being too fat or too thin. Moderation is always the best course. The simple step of losing excess weight can provide numerous health benefits ranging from less aches and pains to avoidance of specific diseases like diabetes. Eating the right foods, such as fruits and vegetables instead of junk foods, can help you have more energy and feel better. Good health is a personal matter, but everyone is different. The advent of personalized medicine is upon us.

Our cities are filled with gyms featuring yoga, aerobics, and Pilates. Services providing weight-loss programs involving exercise and dieting are now multibillion-dollar businesses. This is all good, but there is more that can be done. Convince yourself to be happy, think positively, reduce stress, stay active, and enjoy life. You do not have to go to a gym to exercise. One of the best exercises is walking. It is almost as good as running as far as getting a workout, but without the wear and tear on your body. You can walk upstairs instead of taking an elevator. You can walk on a treadmill or outside in the fresh air on the sidewalk or in a park. You can walk your dog or go shopping. Many suburbanites join a gym and then pay money to someone to rake their leaves, shovel their snow, and mow their lawn. Does that make sense?

I always get a kick out of hearing golfers rave about the beautiful golf courses they have played. Their description of the golf courses verge on ecstatic when describing the elegant greens, the beautiful fairways, the strategically placed trees and sand traps. For those who are not golfers, do not be jealous. Even greater beauty awaits you in local parks, trails, and vast state parks.

Most parks are absolutely free, and provide amusements such as carousels and refreshments from small stands and ice cream trucks. There are bicycle and skateboard lanes. State parks are immense and include camping, bridal paths, and trails leading through thousands of acres of wildflowers and beautiful trees. While golf course fairways and greens are considered beautiful, so too are our neighbors lawns when manicured to perfection and bordered by shrubs and bushes of all kinds. Nature's beauty is everywhere; take time to enjoy it.

If you dig deep enough you may come up with advantages to being a couch potato. Couch potatoes are less likely to injure themselves or even have heart attacks, and they can learn a lot by watching TV. Unfortunately, if you read a lot of books you are called "well read," but if you watch a lot of TV you are not called "well viewed"; you are called a couch potato, a term not held in high regard. So if you care about self-esteem, get off the couch and walk, run, or ride a bicycle for at least one hour a week.

Snacking between meals could actually be a good thing. However, snacking on cake and candy bars is not good, as these sweets should be considered treats, and not the norm. Healthy substitutes are readily available. Nuts are a good alternative. They are full of protein for energy, as are nutrition bars. Many people have changed their habits and have learned to enjoy vegetables, fruits, and yogurt as healthy alternatives to junk food.

There are hundreds of weight-loss diets to choose from. They come from medical organizations, doctors, mothers, and friends. Almost everyone has gone on a diet or two or three. Many diet companies sell foods to go along with dieting suggestions (Weight Watchers, Jenny Craig, NutriSystem). Diets also evolve from theories promoting health (such as benefits of being vegetarian or following the famous "low carb" Scarsdale, Atkins, or South Beach diets, and the "heart healthy" Mediterranean diet). Some people believe in crash diets; addicts go on detox diets. Subway advertises the Subway Diet. There is a diet for everyone.

Since all diets work to a lesser or greater extent, my conclusion is that the best diet is something I would call "The Moderation Diet." You will lose weight if you just decide to go on a diet—any diet. Where there is a will there is a way. Convincing yourself to go on a diet is the first step. If you want to lose weight it does not make any difference which diet you choose, you can just eat less of what you are already eating. You can skip desserts, which can be called a "No Desserts Diet." You can merely switch from soda to water. You can eat the same things you are eating now, but add exercise to your routine. This can be called an "Exercise Diet."

If you set your mind to being happy, you can just as certainly set your mind to losing weight. Whatever diet you are on, believe in it. The one exception is that there are specific diets for people with medical problems. If a doctor prescribes a specific diet, then that is the best diet for you.

Anything taken in excess is a problem. Addiction is often the root of the problem. Smoking cigarettes and drinking alcoholic beverages are two of the major health problems in society. A person who smokes a cigarette for ten minutes is taking approximately ten minutes off his or her life expectancy, and yet people continue to smoke because it is addictive. I know people who have died of lung cancer, and it is terrible to watch their lives disintegrate from a smoking habit they gave up years ago. Electronic cigarettes are a promising phenomenon but the jury is still out as to whether they are as addictive and harmful as cigarettes. The practice of smoking in public venues, buildings, and bars has been seriously curtailed by major municipalities to the point that it has become almost an embarrassment to be seen smoking.

The drinking of alcoholic beverages to excess has been vilified by the publicity given to the many deaths caused by driving under the influence. Police departments throughout the country are enforcing DUI laws through the use of Breathalyzer tests.

Nevertheless, unlike smoking, drinking is held in high esteem by some executives and often glamorized in magazines and motion pictures. The only way that I can think of to reduce alcoholism is to do what was done in the cigarette industry, which introduced filtered, light cigarettes, and now e-cigarettes. Why not pass laws to reduce the alcohol content of beers, wines, and hard liquor? I doubt that drinkers would notice the difference.

Chapter Eleven

What Your Genes Reveal

IMAGINE A LADY IN A BUSINESS SUIT waiting for a train at New York's Grand Central Station. A well-dressed man with a briefcase approaches her, taps her on the shoulder, and says, "I am going to tell you things about yourself that even you do not know. I am going to provide you information that can literally save your life." Astonished by the stranger's comment she replies, "I do not believe it, but you have piqued my interest, please go on." The stranger continued, "Listen carefully to what I have to say because it is important to your well-being. I will answer questions about you that you may not have even considered:

- ▷ What is your ancestry going back 1,000 years or more?

- ▷ Are you predisposed to getting a particular cancer?

- ▷ Which type of diet is most effective for you?

- ▷ Is your general metabolism fast or slow, and specifically how do you react to caffeine?

- ▷ Will you have adverse reactions to foods such as peanuts, gluten, or milk products?

- ▷ Are you predisposed to having high cholesterol or diabetes?

▷ Which drugs are more likely to work for you and which are not?

▷ Are your children more likely to inherit diseases such as Tay-Sachs?

▷ Do you have a proclivity for sports involving endurance or fast-action?

▷ Are the children in your family likely to go bald?

▷ Are you a carrier of genes for recessive diseases?

▷ Do you have an elevated risk for breast cancer or hypertension?

▷ Do you have an increased risk for glaucoma, asthma, or Alzheimer disease?

Shall I go on and . . .?"

The lady interrupts and says, "I do not understand how you can answer those provocative questions without knowing me. But why do I need answers to those questions?" The stranger replies, "Having the answers to those questions can save your life. For example, Angelina Jolie, Sharon Osborne, Kathy Bates, and Christina Applegate learned that they had a predisposition for breast cancer and decided to have double mastectomies. If you were having heart surgery, you might like to know which drugs are more likely to work for you and which are not."

She says "All right, you have convinced me that I should know all that you have described and more. Does this knowledge come from witchcraft? What will it cost to obtain this valuable information and how long will the process take?"

The stranger smiles and says, "It is not witchcraft, it is the latest in medical technology involving the human genome." He explains, "I am a medical doctor trained in the study of genetics. Personal genetic testing has already been assigned medical codes by the FDA so that many of these tests can be covered by your medical plan. Detailed results of your genetic makeup will be given to you in a one hundred–page printout within two weeks."

She succumbs, and asks the doctor to tell her how her genetic makeup can be revealed. He replies, "All you have to do is spit in a tube and all of the information about you will come from an analysis of the DNA in your saliva."

The human genome contains just over twenty thousand genes that are unique to each individual. The effect of genes can be influenced by the environment and other factors including what a person eats, so answers from a personal genetic study cannot be precise. You do not require a prescription to weigh yourself, and now the same is true for a genetic analysis. Finally, on February 22, 2015 the Food and Drug Administration cleared the way for direct to consumer genetic tests for specific diseases. This is a dramatic breakthrough.

There are some people who do not want to know their test results, but the vast majority of people are highly interested in diagnostic procedures that can identify the likelihood of traits and diseases, ranging from obesity to cancer, so that preventive measures may be taken. Depending on the results, choices of prevention can include increased screening, changes in diet or lifestyle or possibly surgery. This knowledge might lead to intelligent planning for long-term care by looking into a suitable nursing home or hospice facility and getting financial affairs in order.

If a child or grandchild has more fast-twitch muscle fibers it would be preferable to be involved in athletic pursuits such as tennis, sprinting, and baseball; if they have more slow-twitch muscle fibers they would be better off in endurance sports such as swimming and long distance running.

If a person is having major heart surgery it would be crucial to know which drugs are more likely to work and at what doses. If someone is contemplating going on a diet they will lose two to three times the weight if the diet is consistent with their genetic makeup. If someone carries a recessive gene for a disease, it would be wise to test a potential spouse's genome to see if it contains the exact same gene for the disease because statistically one out of four children could be afflicted by that disease. And this is only the beginning; the science of personal genomics is developing at an explosive rate. Who knows what else we will be able to learn about ourselves in the next few years through DNA analysis!

A while ago I decided to purchase genetic tests for my immediate family of fourteen people, including a son, two daughters, their three spouses, and my six grandchildren who were very excited to learn about their genetic makeup. They were interested to know which traits were passed on to them by each of their parents and grandparents. About two weeks after saliva samples were mailed in by the family, the results came back via the Internet. My descendants inherited my recessive gene for hemochromatosis, which is a serious disease causing the body to absorb too much iron. Death can result. Fortunately the bad gene has to reside in both parents for this malady to be inherited by a child.

All the blood tests that I have had over the years have indicated low HDL, the good cholesterol. My HDL level was always in the low 30s when it should have been 50 or higher. The genetic results showed that I have a gene for low HDL, so that explains it! Fortunately, I also had a gene for low LDL, the bad cholesterol, and in any case the ratio of overall cholesterol to HDL was always in the proper range. I also had the gene for an increased number of fast twitch muscle fibers, which explains why I have always been a good athlete in team sports. I also have slow metabolism, which explains why I tend to gain weight. The recommended diet to be based on my genes was low-fat, which may explain why I respond better to low fat foods.

Each family member has learned something about inherited genes and the recommended actions that will counteract negative traits. These genetic tests were prepared by *Pathway Genomics* in their own government-approved CLIA laboratory in California. Since my family has benefited from their analyses I decided to invest in the company. There is information on successful investing that is covered in Part 4 of this book, titled "Be More Prosperous."

Advances in healthcare are accelerating on a myriad of fronts, but humans may not benefit from many of these advances for some decades. Sequencing of the human genome began in earnest twenty-five years ago, but the impact on human beings is nascent. Gene mutations are a field in itself. People born with mutated genes may have any one of numerous diseases. For example, sickle cell anemia is the result of a point mutation, a change in just one nucleotide in the gene for hemoglobin. The human genome can be edited to customize the genome of any cell. Correcting gene mutations can eliminate common afflictions, but in the process damage can be done to the afflicted gene or to adjacent genes.

An experiment started in the late 1980s shows enormous potential for fighting disease. The experiment is called CRISPR for short (**C**lustered **R**egularly **I**nterspaced **S**hort **P**alindromic **R**epeats). Researchers at the Hubrecht Institution in the Netherlands showed that with CRISPR they could fix a mutation that causes cystic fibrosis. Companies using CRISPR technology are being formed in several countries. CRISPR appears to be faster and better than existing technologies currently used in gene modification. For some diseases CRISPR would extract blood stem cells from the body and alter and replace them. Technologies like CRISPR may not be ready for intervention in human beings for ten years, but this is an amazing advancement of modern medicine.

It is important for all of us to have an interest in being well-informed about the revolution of healthcare within our lifetime and to be optimistic that there can be a cure for our own health conditions.

Part 3

BE SMARTER

"Human history becomes more and more a race between education and catastrophe." –H.G. Wells

"If Columbus had an advisory committee he would probably still be back at the dock." —Justice Arthur Goldberg

"It wasn't raining when Noah built the ark."
—Howard Ruff

Epiphany

When I was young I wanted to read about sports, adventure, biographies, classic books, philosophy, comics, and cartoons. I reasoned that to do this I needed to read faster and learn mnemonics so I could remember things better. I wanted to do math in my head, faster than others could do it on a slide rule or calculator. So I read books that taught me how to do these things. It has made my life easier and more productive.

Chapter Twelve

Americans Are Not
That Smart

PEOPLE ARE BORN WITH A certain level of intelligence that can only be modestly changed by environment and schooling. For the most part, the brains you are born with are the brains you will take into adult life. Being smart is different than being intelligent. Those imbued with a high IQ can be just as dumb as those with a low IQ—in their careers, family life, and everyday activities. People cannot raise their IQ very much, but they can get smarter through education, learning, and following sound advice.

Children born of wealth often fritter away their riches because of an upbringing that made them dumb. Talented singers such as Justin Bieber, Miley Cyrus, Amy Winehouse, Lindsay Lohan, and Britney Spears have had their lives go off the track because of failures to conform to the norms of society. Meanwhile, smarter singers of lesser talent have built lengthy trouble-free and successful careers. This anomaly holds true as well in other fields such as business, industry, politics, and commerce. If intelligence ruled the world there would be no kings. Money managers and venture capitalists would all be PhDs, and successful politicians would have been at the heads of their college classes.

There are numerous examples of people who exceeded the expectations that their level of education would suggest. Franklin Pierce was last in his college class, but became president of the United States. John McCain was near the bottom of his class at the Naval Academy, but became a war hero, senator, and candidate for president of the United States. General George Armstrong Custer, made famous in "Custer's Last Stand," was last in his class at West Point but became a noted general and war hero. Bill Gates never completed his studies at Harvard University but went on to become an industrial icon by founding Microsoft. George Washington Carver did not have a formal education but became a famous scientist, author, and renowned cotton and peanut farmer earning an honorary doctorate degree from Simpson College. The goal of this chapter is to make you smarter, regardless of your IQ.

To succeed, "It is not what you know but who you know," is a well-known saying that entered common usage one hundred years ago. I would like to tweak it a bit to read this way: To succeed, "it is not what you know, but what *you do not know, that is important.*"

Most people *do not know* the extent to which they can become happier, healthier, smarter, and more prosperous. They *do not know* that they can learn to read faster, memorize better, do math in their head, learn a new profession, join a chorus, obtain a better job, and hundreds of other exciting possibilities. Entrepreneurs, scientists, engineers, biologists, and many others have opened new vistas to mankind by exploring what they *did not know.* In your own way and your own level you can strive to be creative, explore new ventures, have original thoughts, and open your mind to what *you do not know.* Do not stop at what you already know.

Who knows what you can discover when you go beyond what you already know. For example, numerous studies have shown that music training improves the IQs of children. If music training can improve the IQs of children, and make them smarter, what else can open your mind to new ideas and insights? Hopefully, this book will entice you to learn a few tricks that will propel you forward into a better and healthier lifestyle and maybe even improve society.

In building a house, it is necessary to first construct a foundation. In speech making, the subject of the speech must first be mastered through experience and study. In building an army, training comes first. To become smarter, education is required, but not necessarily in a formal manner at high school, vocational school, or college. The very poor, living in the most destitute neighborhoods get smart quickly by learning how to survive in a hostile environment. This is called street smarts, which may be more important than intelligence when it comes to succeeding in any endeavor.

The foundation of a good education is the ability to read. Decades ago, reading was even more important than now because of the advent of high-speed data and video transmission. Today, people who cannot read well can still learn by watching television and videos. Nevertheless, reading is a key factor in becoming smarter, not only by reading books, newspapers, and magazines, but also the directions for such things as putting furniture together or reviewing car manuals.

The United States prides itself on its education system. Yet numerous international studies show that the United States ranks far behind other countries that spend far less per student than we do. According to a 2011 study by *School Library Journal* the United States is ranked 32nd of all countries in mathematical capability and 17th in reading. The *World Fact Book* reports that the United States spends a lofty $810 billion annually on education or $7,743 per school-aged child. The United Kingdom is next at $5,834 and going down the list Russia and Brazil rank 11th and 12th at about $1,750. China spends even less than that per child. While I am not one who believes that the United States has to be number one in world rankings, I do believe we should get more bang for the buck. These troubling international comparisons hold up even after race and economic factors are taken into account.

Since the first one-room schoolhouse was built in the United States in the 1600s, there has been a clamor for better education. The US education system has fallen from first to also-ran. Only a minority of parents are satisfied with the education of their children because of the many flaws in the education system. Despite the best of intentions, federal, state, and local governments have been unable to reverse the downward trend in the international educational rankings of the United States. This is true up through secondary education. Our colleges are still a desirable destination for students throughout the world for educational quality, and also for prestige and necessity to get ahead, since the United States is the most powerful country in the world.

A common defense of the standing of US children is that they are more creative than children in foreign lands. After all, the United States leads the world in technology, innovation, and issuance of patents. But other countries, especially China and India, are catching up, and their GNPs are currently growing at three times that of the United States. It has been said that the 20th century was ruled by the United States, the 19th century by England and the 18th century by Europe. At this time there is strong evidence that the 21st century will be led by a country other than the United States—perhaps by China.

In a 2014 report, the National Science Board warns that the predominance of the United States in science and technology is fading, due partly to federal cutbacks in research and development. In the past decade, global research spending in the United States has declined from 37 percent to 30 percent, while the share of research done by Asian countries has grown from 25 percent to 34 percent. Remarkably, the share of global research done by China increased from 2 percent to 15 percent in the same time period. In recognition of that fact, I have some suggestions as to how to improve our education system.

The cornerstones of our elementary school education are the three R's, the tongue in cheek abbreviations for readin', rightin', and 'rithmatic. There are important changes that can be made in the teaching of reading, writing, and arithmetic. First, we should add the study of mnemonics to aid in memory retention and to expand the minds of students. Second, we need to highlight speed in reading and arithmetic. Third, we should teach arithmetic in new ways that amuse and entertain students. Arithmetic is a lot of fun if taught in the correct way. Many students, especially young girls, have a fear of arithmetic; this does not have to be so if it taught correctly. I have studied speed-reading, speed math, and mnemonics, and it has helped me tremendously in school, business, and everyday life.

Our children are not getting dumber. Children in foreign countries are getting smarter faster. The American education system has failed to keep pace with other countries. This deficiency is not due to a lack of funding, so throwing more money at the problem will not work. As (Leroy) Satchel Paige (US baseball player 1906-1982), the great black baseball pitcher said, "*Do not look back. Something may be gaining on you.*"

Both individuals and corporations have initiated programs to improve our education system. Most recently, Intel has announced that it will invest $300 million to sponsor STEM education in K-12 classes and in universities. STEM stands for **S**cience, **T**echnology, **E**ngineering, and **M**athematics. This effort should help budding child superstars attain their goals for careers in science and technology. More companies should help get our education system out of the rut that it is in.

One reason that I am happy all the time is that I have no back-log. I read everything the day it is received, including newspapers, magazines, business plans, emails, catalogues, and legal briefs. Having no backlog eliminates stress and allows me to be happy every day.

Every reader of this book can easily learn the basics of getting smarter from the best and easiest ways to learn to read faster and to learn mathematical skills and teach these to their children and grandchildren.

Chapter Thirteen

The Key to Being Smarter Is Reading Faster

WHY IS THERE A DISPARITY between educational spending and results? I have an answer that seems obvious and it can be summed up in three words: TEACH MENTAL SPEED. Let me explain by a personal experience. I was always a fast reader, and that helped me become a good student.

One day, perhaps fifty years ago, I attended a class called Evelyn Wood Reading Dynamics®. A class of about forty students was tested on day one for speed and comprehension. I do not remember my exact speed on the initial test, but it was approximately 500 words per minute. I do remember that I scored the highest mark in comprehension based on a reading test. At the end of the course my reading speed was clocked at 4,000 words per minute, and I still had the highest comprehension in the class. An explanatory note: I did not read a newspaper or a book at 4,000 words per minute: I read a story of several pages at a rate of 4,000 words per minute. I am a very competitive person, so given a test in class I will ace it.

For a while I read everything speedily by moving my index finger horizontally across the page and then diagonally down the page a few lines at a time, using the *Evelyn Wood* system, which is to first read three lines, and then read five lines diagonally at a time, and finally read straight down the middle of the page. I learned an important lesson, namely that it was possible to read and absorb written material a lot faster than I imagined.

More profoundly, the lesson I learned was not only that I could read fast, but that my brain could be pushed to operate at a higher level. In college, if I had two final examinations, one at nine a.m. and one at eleven a.m., I would read the entire textbook for the first test an hour beforehand and do the same for the second test. Again, please understand, I do not read 4,000 words per minute all the time, only when needed.

For example, when I go to the office and have to leave for an appointment in fifteen minutes I read the *Wall Street Journal* before leaving. I do not read nearly as fast when I am enjoying breakfast or reading a book of poetry or science.

One of my lawyers recently noticed that I read legal briefs very quickly. He said that he reads at a speed of approximately 200 wpm and asked me how I could read so fast. My first thought was that his reading pace had cost me money, but then I explained my theory which is as follows: school children read at speeds that are comfortable to them. Angela Chen of Dow Jones states that seven-year-olds read about 80 words a minute and sixth graders read about 185 words a minute, while the average college graduate reads about 250 words per minute. Regardless of the speed at which people read, they can learn to read faster.

Teachers accept that children read at different speeds and do nothing about it. It seems that our educational system does not give children enough credit. A child first learns to walk before it can run. Given a certain level of physical ability, if a child practices running enough he or she may join a track team. With enough practice the child could potentially compete in the Olympics. Why not the same progression in reading? I believe that the brains of children can be lazy and have to be pushed to reach their potential.

Why accept the fact that one child only reads at 200 wpm and another child reads at two or three times that rate? It may take some practice, just as with the sport of running, but everyone can learn to read faster. With the advent of computers, cursors can be manipulated to move down the screen at progressively faster speeds to prod children to read faster. How is it that an Evelyn Wood Reading Dynamics® class can increase reading speeds for all attendees after a few hours of training? There are many other schools and online programs that can accomplish the same thing.

In reading, as in all endeavors, slowness can cost money. A plumber or electrician that works slowly because of lack of skills and experience may take two hours to fix a problem instead of one hour. You pay more for this. The same is true for lawyers and accountants, or for any service that charges on an hourly basis.

No one enjoys waiting in line at a movie theatre, bank, or airline. Businesses give a lot of thought and ingenuity to reducing waiting times—ranging from simply adding windows to sophisticated advanced ticket purchase systems. Airlines allow handicapped passengers to board first, and so on. How about giving some attention to speeding up something that is much more important: reading? Let us enable everyone to read faster, especially children.

Did you ever notice someone on a crowded train or subway reading a newspaper? It could take almost as long to turn the page than for someone else to read a page. A fast reader will always have his thumb and forefinger at the top of the page ready to flip to the next page. Such small attention to detail could speed up reading by 10 percent or more.

A speed-reader can read a book in a day or a week rather than a month. Speed-readers are more likely to be smarter than slow readers because they are absorbing more information. Children and adults should be encouraged to take Internet courses in speed-reading. It would be beneficial to students and professional business people alike. In the United States the answer to low international rankings in reading and mathematics has been to throw money at the problem. This solution has not fixed the problem one bit. The focus should not be on spending more, but on improving the current education system. Of course there are obstacles to over-come—satisfaction with the status quo, union reluctance to deal with something new, and the inability to fire poor teachers.

I have taken numerous courses outside of the formal educa-tion system of high school and college. Isn't it odd how much can be learned in individual courses taken in night school, especially licensing courses for real estate, insurance, accounting, and finance. Many independent courses are for mere hours rather than days, weeks, and months in formal education.

Friends who have taken courses in everything from automotive repair to classical music appreciation become quite knowledgeable in those specific fields. Instead of sitting at home and whining about an inability to appreciate life or find a job, more people should get up from the couch and take one or more of the abundant courses available in person or on a computer through the Internet. A formal education is fine, but if you want to get smarter, consider taking specific classes outside the formal system for fun, knowledge, and career development.

Oh, the joys of reading faster! It makes you smarter, reduces stress, gives you more free time, and advances your career. A com-mon problem for many people is a huge backlog of reading mate-rial. Some people have a bad habit of saving articles and books with the intention of catching up on their reading someday. Backlog equals stress. Either throw out the backlog or learn how to read faster.

As a Wall Street securities analyst covering numerous public companies, and as a venture capitalist invested in as many as thirty companies at one time, I receive financial reports, updates, and proposals every day from companies and public relation firms. Moreover, to keep abreast of the technology industry, I have to read numerous technology and financial magazines. On top of that there are company lawsuits involving hundreds of pages of documentation and testimony.

Also, in the financial industry, the *Wall Street Journal* and *New York Times* are must-reads. It would be easy to fall behind and have mounds of paper everywhere on my desk or in file cabinets. Instead I read everything, including hundreds of emails, the day they are received. I also have plenty of time to enjoy my family, play softball on Sunday, and read several good books a month. No backlog means less stress. I am not saying this to boast; I am telling you this to convince you that reading faster could change your life. Absorbing information by reading, listening, or watching media events is an essential part of our lives. Read faster, not only because you must, but because you can.

We live in a faster world. Airplanes fly faster, trains have become high-speed, cars travel faster, highways have higher speed limits, and information flows thousands of times faster than letters via high-speed broadband data communications. Who needs encyclopedias when information can be retrieved almost instantaneously through search engines provided by Google, Microsoft, and Yahoo? Humans enjoy the fruits of what technology has created. Human intelligence has failed to keep up with the abundant capabilities of the human mind. We have to return to basics—reading faster, doing math faster, and improving our memories. It can and must be done to maintain our preeminence in the world.

Speed-reading is now being offered by numerous companies as apps for mobile devices and computers. In-person speed reading classes such as Evelyn Wood are available in many communities. The company Iris Reading LLC also holds in-person courses for speed-reading. Many cities offer speed-reading courses in their night schools and colleges. Every course has its own unique method of teaching speed-reading. The techniques involve skimming and absorbing thoughts, concepts, or groups of words at one time. A few apps are free and others charge by the minute, month, or course.

Here is an alphabetical list of a few companies that offer online courses and/or reading apps. I am not recommending any particular course because that is a choice for the reader.

Fastreaders

Iris Reading LLC

Outread (app for iOS)

Plympton, Inc.

Rev It Up Reading

RocketReader

Speed Reader X

Speed Reading Online

Spritz Technology Inc.

Spreeder.com (a free service offered by 7-Speed-Reading™)

By the time this book is published, the apps available will have changed and many other companies will enter the fray. Reading habits are being changed to fit the needs of people with mobile devices. People on the go are now used to reading in short bursts, and technologies are being developed to satisfy their needs. The only danger is that too much of a "Cliff Notes" approach to reading may not be as good, powerful, or detailed as the traditional approach to reading. Once in a while you might want to slow down (for instance if you are reading a poem), but at least you will have a choice of good reading skills.

Chapter Fourteen

Reading Extensively Will Improve Writing

SKILL IN WRITING IS SUBJECTIVE and hard to measure. Writing a novel requires a vivid imagination; technical writing comes from extensive knowledge, and all writing evolves from extensive reading. It used to be that children were born to read, but nowadays they may be born to play games and communicate via instant messaging on mobile devices.

In recent years newspaper circulation has declined precipitously, and bookstores have disappeared in great numbers. Yet reading has not become a lost art. People are now reading more and more on portable devices such as computers, iPads, and e-book readers. Meanwhile, children and adults still keep diaries and logs. Digital messages have proliferated on social service networks like Facebook and Twitter. In the 21st century, the form may be different, but the printed message lives on despite the onslaught of digital communications.

Books in print are giving way to digital books, but more books are being published today than ever before. Self-publishing is growing rapidly while traditional book publishing is declining just as fast. Thus a graph showing the trend in publishing is in the shape of an X. Reading is not a lost art and neither is writing, but change permeates the publishing industry.

But is good writing in danger of becoming a lost art? Will lovely handwritten letters on personalized stationary be replaced by instant messaging replete with abbreviations and cute images like smiley faces? Does receiving a message with the salutation ILY make the heart beat faster as much as the salutation I love you?

I was a voracious reader when I was a child as young as four. I liked reading the comics and the sports pages as well as books from the public library. I went to a technical high school followed by a science and engineering track in college and a finance-oriented track in grad school. No liberal arts for me, so I never studied grammar. Nevertheless, I learned to write well because I had a feel for writing based on all the reading I did.

While working on Wall Street I wrote thousands of research reports for three of the six leading investment-banking firms. The editors in each of those firms told me that they never had to edit my work. Many other top securities analysts were as smart as could be but needed extensive editing of their reports. I have written dozens of articles in leading publications that hardly needed editing even though I do not know a gerund from a past participle. Somehow I learned how to write.

My advice to parents and grandparents is to acquire books for their children to read for sheer enjoyment. At first children should read for fun. Eventually in school they will study fine literature not only for enjoyment but to admire excellence in writing. The path to good writing is through extensive reading. After all, reading is fun, educational, and inspiring. It is okay for children to play games on handheld devices, but it is not a substitute for reading. An e-book reader would be a perfect gift for a child because it would encourage reading.

Many schools encourage students to write essays. Obviously, this is good, but writing can also be taught at home. Have your children and grandchildren write greeting cards, thank you cards, and letters to their cousins, friends, and even to their siblings. Tell them if they want something from you they might get it if they wrote you a nice letter. Spelling errors are abundant at a young age, but this is the only way that spelling is learned when you are young.

Older children can be taught to write articles for local newspapers even if they are never published. Many children enjoy writing but they need encouragement and ideas for topics. Writing is fun, but is also essential in crafting a resume for employment. Children should be taught to understand that everything they enjoy—music, cartoons, TV programs, books, and magazines—are written by people who are making money doing what they love. This may inspire children to write for the enjoyment of others.

Writing and baseball, how do they go together? I will tell you. When I go to a baseball game with a youngster who plays little league baseball, he enjoys the game, but there is also something to learn. If the youngster plays third base, I advise him to watch not the ballgame but the third baseman. How he positions himself against different hitters. How he gets relay throws from the outfielder. How he tags out runners. How he starts double plays. It is the same with writing; details are important.

Both adults and children read books for enjoyment, but do they analyze sentence construction, the use of conjunctions and punctuations? Those who want to become writers should circle exceptional sentences and paragraphs that are magical, inspirational, and, at the same time, easy to read. Adopt a style that fits you. Learn how to use descriptive adjectives and adverbs. Have a child describe a person fully by including descriptions of clothing, attitude, energy, posture, and persona. These techniques help develop writing ability.

An even more important element of writing ability comes from inspiration. From my experience, school essays generally involve copying a few sentences or phrases from one book and a few more from another book. A style of writing is not emphasized.

For those interested in writing for a living, there are numerous classes given by excellent professionals with backgrounds as authors and editors who know how to write novels, screen plays, non-fiction works, and the like. Adult education classes in writing abound. The best writers continue to hone their craft by reading works by their peers.

Fortunately, many universities offer free online writing courses while other universities charge for the service. If you know your stuff you may want to write an article in the local newspaper; you might even decide you want to become a reporter.

Writing takes many forms, and in all forms it is a vital contributor to success in social life and in business. Socially, it is helpful to write simple thank you notes with a flair that will earn respect. Students who write interesting essays get higher grades, and to get into college, strong essays are a necessity. Technical writing requires compactness and expert knowledge of the subject. Postings on Facebook and tweets on Twitter can be read by millions of people if you are famous or want to be famous. Everyone seems to want to write a great novel, but few have the necessary tools to be successful.

An excellent way to express your thoughts and show your expertise on any subject is to author a blog. A blog is a website that offers personal opinions that many others have an interest in accessing. A blog is not a one-time thing; it is regularly updated. Experts provide their thoughts on subjects as diverse as sports, cooking, politics, cosmetics, and finance. Popular blogs have launched many successful careers. Blogs can be offered free or for a monthly fee.

In many ways, blogs have become the "new" magazine articles. There are many services that facilitate blogging; one called Blogger is offered by Google.

As your capabilities and experience improve, you may want to write articles for major magazines. Every item in the thousands of catalogues delivered to your home or office is described by someone in a distinct and compact manner. Every ad on TV is written by someone; every formal speech given by the president of the United States is written by a speechwriter and shown on a teleprompter; every TV sitcom, Broadway play or movie has a screenwriter.

The written word is everywhere, so you may as well learn how to write properly for social occasions and for business. The writing process starts with reading, learning grammar, and gaining experience. Children learn a spoken language at the age of two or three; they can also learn to read and write at a very early age. Make sure that happens. The greatest philosophers of the world, over the past three thousand years, are known by what they scribbled on paper. *The Dead Sea Scrolls* and *The Diary of Anne Frank* are known to millions of people. Your diary may be just as important to your family. Writing is important and could be eternal.

Chapter Fifteen

How to Do Math
in Your Head, Really

IF YOU ARE NOT INTERESTED IN MATH, feel free to skip this chapter. But if you do so you will be missing out on a few exciting and simple tricks. Arithmetic, mathematics, trigonometry, geometry, and calculus are words that strike fear into the hearts of innocent children and mature adults. Arithmetic is the part of mathematics that can be handled by a simple calculator. Mathematics is all encompassing, involving complex symbols and proofs covering trigonometry, geometry, and calculus. Engineering, science, and physics are built on a foundation of mathematics.

For the great majority of people, simple math is all that is needed to succeed in life and in business. Cooking, buying, selling, making change, traveling abroad, keeping score, statistical analysis—all of these things can be done with a knowledge of simple arithmetic. Sports fans are bathed in statistics such as batting averages in baseball, yards per carry in football, and team statistics in basketball. People who may have hated math in school feel quite comfortable following statistics in the sports they love, which brings me to the conclusion that math need not be feared if taught in a way both practical and interesting to students.

There are students interested in cooking, others in sports, and still others in business. Connecting these students with the intersection of math and their specific interest is a way to eliminate the fear of math that may have been passed on by their parents. Kids should be taught that math is fun. Concepts like long division, fractions, and decimals should not be taught until children have a firm grasp of the benefits derived from these concepts.

For example, do school children know that baseball batting and pitching averages are based on decimals and fractions? Do they know that a batting average of 300 is really a decimal of 0.300 (meaning 300 out of 1,000) or a fraction equaling three-tenths? Do they know that the food cooked by their parents is based on recipes involving measurements and temperatures, which is all about math? Do they know that the ingredients of foods for sale at supermarkets are listed in order of volume? For example, if sugar is the first ingredient listed, the product has more sugar than anything else. If a bag of trail mix is purchased, read the ingredients to see which is the most used ingredient: peanuts or raisins, etc.

In college, I studied the highest levels of math, including calculus and differential equations, but was never properly taught how to use what I studied in practical situations. Therefore, to this day, I do not use calculus very much in situations where it could be used. Looking back I wish that the professors first taught me the uses of calculus before they taught me the specifics of calculus.

In chapter 12 I talked about the basics of getting smarter. Reading was the key attribute to getting smarter. In math the key attribute to getting better at math is understanding arithmetic. Becoming good at arithmetic will lead to success in algebra, geometry, and trigonometry. In this chapter you will learn simple ways to do math in your head and astound your friends about how smart you are. Your brain can be as fast as any computer and can certainly operate faster than pencil and paper or a calculator.

As I said, math is fun. Let me demonstrate it by a few simple tricks involving the number 9, which is a magical and fascinating number. Hold out your two hands palms up. Number the fingers from one to ten from left to right. To multiply a one-digit number by nine, just bend the finger representing the number to be multiplied. For example, to multiply 3 × 9, bend the third (middle) finger into your palm, and you will see that two fingers to the left of the bent finger remain, as do seven fingers to the right of the bent finger, which provides the answer 27. To multiply 6 × 9, bend the sixth finger (this is the pinky of the right hand) to obtain the answer 54; the five fingers of the left hand represent five and the four fingers to the right of the bent finger representing four.

Another trick is to ask a child his or her favorite (or least favorite) number. If it is 7, multiply 63 × 12345679 on a calculator. The answer will be all sevens. How is this done? The 12345679 is always the number that will be multiplied. Notice that the number 8 is omitted. The first digit of the other number is one less than the favorite number 7 (which is 6) and the second digit is whatever adds up to 9, and in this case it is 3. For another example, to get an answer of all 4s just multiply 12345679 by 36.

A way to obtain a string of identical numbers is to divide any three or four digit number by 9. The remainders, which are the decimals after the decimal point, will be a series of identical digits. Sometimes the remainder will be a string of zeros, such as dividing 999 by 9. So, a calculator will show no remainder at all, just all zeros. This trick works also for dividing five and eight-digit numbers by 9. Does it work for numbers of even more digits? What is there about the magical number 9?

Now ask someone to write down a three-digit number and tell you the digits as they are writing it down. Ask them to divide by 9 and to not tell you the answer as to what the remainder is (the digits after the decimal point). If they tell you the number is 521, before they can calculate the answer, you quickly add up the digits and shout out that the remainders are all 8s. In this case, the digits 521 add up to 8. If the number were 658, adding up the digits comes to 19 and by casting out 9s the remainder is 1. So the remainder in that example would be all 1s.

Here is another trick, write down the number 0 on a piece of paper and put the piece of paper in your pocket. Have someone write down a four-digit number, mix up the digits any way they want, and write down the mixed up digits as a second number. Subtract the smaller number from the larger number and divide the result by 9. Pull out the piece of paper and show them that you magically predicted that the remainder would be 0. The answer is always a whole number with nothing left over as a remainder.

Have a person write down three digits in decreasing order, like 542, 651, or 871. Reverse the digits of the number and subtract it from the first set of digits. For example, if 542 were selected, subtract the reverse number 245 and get 297 (542 − 245 = 297). Then reverse the answer 297 to get 792. Next add 297 + 792 to equal 1089. Notice that after numbers are reversed and added, the answers of 297 and 792 always have a 9 in the middle, and the two outside digits always add up to 9. The final answer of 1,089 will always be the answer regardless of which three digits were chosen initially. Try it yourself using any three-digit number to start.

Let us move on from fun with the number 9, although there are many more interesting things to do with the number 9. Children have to be taught how much fun math can be and how useful math is in everyday life, such as buying things in stores and getting back change. Knowledge of math can even save money. For example, a family of six enters a pizza shop to buy a pizza to be shared by everyone. Here is where knowledge of math can save money for the family. On the menu is an 8-inch pizza selling for eight dollars and a 12 inch pizza selling for twelve dollars. Which is more economical for the family to purchase? The answer can be found in a simple formula $A = \pi r^2$ which measures the area in square inches of a circle. π (pi) is a constant, which is approximately 3.14, and r is the radius—the distance from the center of the pizza to the edge. Let us round π to 3 to simplify the multiplication. An 8-inch pizza has a radius of half of 8 inches, or 4 inches. So 3×4^2 (16) is 48 square inches; compare that to a 12-inch pizza that has an area of 3×6^2 (36) or 108 square inches. The larger pizza has more than double the area of the smaller pizza. To be exact, the larger pizza is 125 percent (188 ÷ 48) larger than the smaller pizza. If you pay 50 percent more for the larger pizza you are getting way more pizza for the money.

For older children or adults, a mathematician named Salman Khan has come up with ingenious ways to make mathematics entertaining and easy to learn. In the space of a year Mr. Khan attracted more than 3 million people to his website. His system, which has gained a high level of popularity, should be embraced by school systems throughout the United States. Math teachers should teach from the videos of Salman Khan, founder of the Khan Academy, a free online education platform that has produced thousands of online videos focused on mathematics.

Besides Khan there are numerous, innovative math books as opposed to the same old math books that have been around for sixty years. Many years ago I read a book called *The Trachtenberg Speed System of Basic Mathematics* and have enjoyed reading a plethora of mathematical books since. Another book I enjoyed is

Vedic Mathematics Made Easy by Dhaval Bathia; it is very intriguing. These books and numerous others unlock the secrets of speed math and make mathematics fun to do. Children will appear to be so-called math geniuses if they follow the videos in Kahn's Academy and learn to read and enjoy appropriate age-related books on arithmetic and mathematics.

Doing math in your head is easy if you learn a few simple tricks. I use these tricks in everyday life and particularly in business. Let us start with something as simple as multiplying a two-digit number by 11. The normal way of multiplying two digit numbers is as follows:

How to multiply a two-digit number by 11 in your head

34	62	11	84
× 11	× 11	× 11	× 11
34	62	11	84
34	62	11	84
3⑦4	6⑧2	1②1	924

Look at the answers. All you have to do to get the answer to the first three examples is to add the two digits that are multiplied by 11 and place it in the middle. In the fourth example, on the right hand side of the page, addition of the middle digits are larger than ten (in this case 12) so a 1 is carried to increase the first digit from an 8 to a 9. Without further explanation, you should be able to instantaneously know the answer of multiplying any two-digit number by 11.

Multiplying 11 by a three-digit number is also easy to do in your head. Look at the examples below.

How to multiply a three-digit number by 11 in your head

243	451	232	255	672
× 11	× 11	× 11	× 11	× 11
243	451	232	255	672
243	451	232	255	672
2673	4961	2552	2805	7392

The three examples on the left do not require a carry, so it is very easy to do in your head. At all times the leftmost digit is the left most digit in the answer. The right most digit is always the right most digit in the answer. It is the two middle digits that require just a little bit of brain work. Add the two left most digits and that becomes the second digit of the answer. Add the two right most digits and that becomes the third digit of the answer. The two examples on the right side require a carry of 1 to the digits on the left.

The fun of being able to do multiplications swiftly in your head is satisfying and exciting. If you multiply a number by 12, use the eleven trick and add the number being multiplied. So if $11 \times 23 = 253$, to multiply by 12 just add 23 to 253 to arrive at the answer of 276.

A simple way to multiply random 2-digit numbers is to multiply by the nearest round number and then multiply by the remaining number. For example, if you multiply 26×32, in your head you can multiply 20×32, which is 640, and then multiply 6×32, which is 192, and add the two together to get 832.

Let us say you want to multiply 35 × 35 or 55 × 55 as shown below:

Squaring a 2-digit number ending in 5

35	55
× 35	× 55
175	275
105	275
1225	3025

Look at the answers. You can get those answers as shown above, or you can do it on a calculator. I do it in my head by using a very simple trick. The last two digits are always 25 when squaring a 2-digit number ending in 5. The first two digits can be easily calculated in your head by multiplying the first digit by a number that is 1 higher. In the first example above just multiply the first digit 3 by 4 and you get 12, which are the first two digits, so the full answer is 1225.

Let me give you another example. One day I multiplied 49 × 51 and found that the answer was one less than 50 × 50 (2,500), so I experimented. I found that 48 × 52 was four less than 50 × 50 and 47 × 53 was nine less than multiplying 50 × 50. Aha! To multiply a number that is equally above and below another, the answer can be found by subtracting the square of the number from the central number. For example 30 × 30 is 900, 29 × 31 is 1 less than 900, 28 × 32 is 4 less than 900, 27 × 33 is 9 less and 26 × 34 is 16 less or 884. Get the picture? The answer is the square of the difference from the mean.

The same system applies to other 2 digit numbers equidistant from a central number. If you multiply 57 × 53 you know the answer is going to be four less than 55 × 55, and we already explained that 55 × 55 is 3025, so the answer is going to be 3021. It is harder to multiply 26 × 28, but you know the answer is going to be one less than 27 × 27.

Now let us look at a shortcut to multiplying high two digit numbers; for example, 88 × 95 = 8360. How do I multiply that almost instantly in my head? Take the difference of each number to 100; this is called the complement.

$$
\begin{array}{r}
88 \\
\times\ 95 \\
\hline
8360
\end{array}
\quad
\begin{array}{l}
\text{(12 is the complement to 100)} \\
\text{(\ 5 is the complement to 100)}
\end{array}
$$

The complement of 88 is 12 while the complement of 95 is 5. To get the last two digits of the answer, multiply the two complements and get 60. The first two digits are either of the original numbers minus the complement of the other number, so 95 less 12 is 83. Oddly enough the same answer for the first two digits can be calculated by using the other original number, because 88 less 5 also equals 83. Isn't this fun? If you know a lot of math tricks you can do multiplication in your head faster than anyone can do with a calculator. This is not a mathematics book, so I am not going to go into other fascinating tricks to do in your head. Wouldn't it be fun to have your children learn these tricks and challenge you to who would be faster, the child doing it in his head or you doing it with a calculator?

There are hundreds of ways to do calculations in your head. Since I am not going to make this a book on math, if you are interested in learning more about this, you can read one of the many books on mental calculations available in the library, for purchase in a bookstore, or on–line at Amazon.

Chapter Sixteen

Simple Tricks
for a Better Memory

How would you like to:

- ▷ be able to remember things better?

- ▷ accomplish twenty errands without preparing a list?

- ▷ give a speech without notes?

- ▷ get an "A" on tests?

- ▷ go to a business meeting totally informed and well-prepared?

- ▷ remember a phone number without writing it down?

- ▷ order food for all in your party by hearing their orders once?

I have done all of those things and more because I have studied mnemonics. You can do some or all of the things I can do and it only takes a little study and some experience to hone your capabilities.

One of the underlying concepts of mnemonics (the art of remembering) is that people will more readily learn things in which they are interested. Therefore, teachers should develop interest and excitement in the subjects they teach before getting into the learning process. The result will be smarter children who are eager to learn. It is evident that a man and a woman walking along a city street will remember different things they have seen. A man will likely remember a window display of a sporting goods store, while a woman will more easily remember a dress shop window display. Develop an interest in a subject before teaching the subject.

Some people say they do not have a good memory, yet can remember sporting events that happened thirty years ago, vividly recalling baseball games they saw decades ago. Others can remember economic statistics and successful stock trades made many years ago. There are those who remember children's birthdays, the first day their grandchildren walked, or first lost a tooth. The truth is that everyone has the capability of having a good memory and improving it. Yet, mnemonics, a vital aspect of learning, is ignored by the education system.

Teachers teach and pupils learn, but they also forget some of what they have learned. The science of mnemonics is more than just tricks; it is about helping people, young and old, retain what they have learned. Mnemonics involves concentration, focus, and stretching the mind to increase the ability to learn. Once you open your mind to learning new things you will be amazed at the expansion of your thought process. Laboratory assistants learn from their mentors about such things as stem cells and viruses and then go on to win Nobel prizes because they have eagerly absorbed information with minds that were open to making exciting discoveries.

Many people use mnemonic techniques without giving it a thought. There is a cute poem for remembering the days in a month:

Thirty days hath September, April, June, and November;

February has twenty-eight alone.

All the rest have thirty-one

Except in Leap Year; that's the time

When February's Days are twenty-nine.

Being adept at mnemonics I remember how many days in a month by the short expression Junapseptembernovember30. When remembering phrases such as "feed a fever, starve a cold" you will only get confused if you try to remember both. Just learn one phrase, not both; for example, feed a fever. If you remember that phrase and someone asks you what to do about a cold, you will remember that the maxim is not to feed it but to starve it. If you try to remember both sides of the rule, you are more likely to mix them up.

A mnemonic device to remember the names of the Great Lakes is to use the acronym HOMES, which stands for Huron, Ontario, Michigan, Erie, and Superior. There are handy mnemonic techniques for remembering elements of grammar. For example, put "i" before "e" except after "c," with another exception for these words: either, seized, neither, weird, and leisure, or for words sounding like 'a,' as in neighbor and weigh." These mnemonic devices are useful and easy to remember.

If you study mnemonics you will learn a lot more than a few cute poems or phrases. You will learn how to concentrate which is one of the basic tenets of mnemonics. To sharpen one's focus, an author advised sitting under a tree and just thinking about the number four, nothing else, for thirty minutes.

When I attended college I employed mnemonics for just about everything. I would make an acronym out of the first letters of key phrases describing the six reasons for the Civil War. Another time I made a chain of words out of the five events precipitating civil rights legislation. The chain of words I would make for occasions like this would be a phrase or sentence that I could remember or even an easy flow from one word to the next.

There is no end to the usefulness of mnemonic techniques. Many decades ago I read a fascinating book by Bruno Furst called *Stop Forgetting*. Since the Bruno Furst book many authors have jumped on the mnemonic bandwagon. Any and all of these books are a good read and beneficial. A feature in almost all books on mnemonics is the ability to remember one hundred things in any order and to recite them back in any order. This system can be taught to almost anyone in less than an hour. In fact, it can be taught in ten minutes and then it is just a matter of practice.

Before learning how to remember one hundred things in any order, let me describe a learning experience I had with some of my grandchildren. To improve and sharpen their capabilities, I decided to have them remember ten things in random order.

Early one day three of my grandchildren, ages eight to eleven, who were sleeping over, came into the kitchen one at a time to eat breakfast. I challenged each of them to recall ten things that I would list for them, in any order, by linking a picture of those things with ten objects in my kitchen. Going from left to right the objects in the kitchen, which form what I call the master list, are shown below on the left side. The master list never changes. The ten things to remember always change and are shown on the right side.

I instructed the children to remember the numerical sequence of the kitchen objects surrounding them. They were free to observe the ten kitchen objects during the test, starting with the refrigerator in the corner of the room and proceeding clockwise. Then I gave them the list of ten things shown on the next page to remember.

Master List	Things to Remember
1. Refrigerator	Tree
2. Coffee maker	Car
3. Microwave	Policeman
4. Sink	Table
5. Window	Book
6. Door	Shoe
7. Stove	Glass
8. Broom Closet	Rug
9. Cupboard	Bird
10. Chair	Quilt

Each child was easily able to remember the ten things by associating them with the ten objects in the kitchen. That was the easy part. The real test came the next morning to see if they still remembered the ten items in any order.

The next morning, the three gathered in the kitchen for breakfast and were given a surprise test. I said "What is number three?" They spied the microwave unit and shouted almost in unison "policeman!" I asked them what picture they created in their mind. Each of the children made an association using a different image. One saw the policeman in the microwave unit, one saw the policeman seizing the microwave to take it away, and the last child saw the policeman standing on top of the microwave unit. I think you get the idea. Needless to say, the three grandchildren remembered all ten items in random order and were proud of it.

Memory by association is as easy as combining two pictures into one, one picture from the master list and one of the items to be remembered. The more ridiculous the picture formed in your mind, the easier it is to remember the item. The master list is the key to remembering things in any order. You can do this with the objects around the living room or any room in the house.

Let us go further and instruct you on how to remember one hundred things in any order. It is just as simple as remembering ten things once you establish the master list. Here is how it is done. Numbers 0–9 are assigned the sounds of consonants.

1. "T" is one downward stroke so the sound of "t" or "th" is **1**.

2. "N" is two downward strokes so the sound of "n" is **2**.

3. "M" is three downward strokes so the sound of "m" is **3**.

4. "R" is the last letter of four so the sound of "r" is **4**.

5. "L" is the Roman numeral for fifty so the sound of "L" is **5**.

6. "J" is a backward six so the sounds of "j", "ch", "sh", "tch", or "dg" is **6**.

7. "K," when looking at the right side of the K, is a backward 7, so the sound of "k" or "hard c" is **7**.

8. "F" is written like the number eight when it is written as a lowercase script letter with circular loops, so the sound of "*f*", "v", or "ph" is **8**.

9. "P" looks like a backwards nine so the sound of "p" or "b" is **9**.

0. "Z" is the first letter of zero so the sound of "z", "s", or "a soft c" is the number **0**.

The master list of ten sounds does not involve vowels, only consonants. These ten sounds are translated into one hundred words, which you must make into vivid pictures in your mind. All you have to do to remember one hundred items is to memorize ten sounds and their corresponding numbers. Carry this list with you and look at it when someone gives you the task of remembering one hundred or fewer items. You will use word pictures 1–20 much more often than the higher numbers because it is normally not necessary to remember more than twenty items. An abbreviated list would look like this:

1. T, Th

2. N

3. M

4. R

5. L

6. J, Ch

7. K, C

8. F, V

9. B, P

0. S, Z

A Quick Test:

What is your word for 7?

What is your word for 17?

What is your word for 25?

What is your word for 33?

What is your word for 62?

What is your word for 71?

What is your word for 99?

My answers are on page 133.

The next step is to create and memorize vivid pictures of the one hundred words that you have constructed from the preceding list. While I offer my own list of word pictures, you can use any word pictures that suit you. On page 133 is a list of the one hundred word pictures that I use to remember one hundred items in any order. By the way, I can shout the list of one hundred words in my master list as fast as you can count out loud the numbers from one to one hundred.

It may be best to remember your list of word pictures numbered one to ten first, and after mastering those ten pictures proceeding to master eleven to nineteen, and so on, remembering ten word pictures at a time until you can instantly recall the picture related to all numbers from one to one hundred.

Practice by having someone say "seven," and you should immediately say "key" or whatever picture is in your mind for seven. If someone says "nine" you should immediately say "bee" or whatever picture you have in your mind for nine. It comes down to this: if you want to be able to remember one hundred items in any order and recite them back in any order, you first have to immediately recall the pictures in your master list.

Notice that "T" is the first letter of 1 and the first letter for 10 to 19 as well. "T" is also the last letter in 21, 31, 41, 51, 61, 71, 81, and 91. In a similar manner "N" is used for 2 on the master list and is the first letter in words 21–29. The pictures that I associate with numbers 1 to 100 are on page 133. One is a tee used in golf to support a golf ball. If I am presented with a list of one hundred items, and the first item on the list is a microwave oven, I imagine the microwave oven on top of the tee, and I am hitting it with a golf club. Two is Noah standing in front of the ark, observing animals boarding the boat two at a time. Whatever item is given to me as number 2, I imagine sitting atop a horse, for example.

The more bizarre the picture you imagine the easier it will be to remember the item you are given to remember. If someone gives me a list of one hundred items to remember and number 13 is my boss, I would imagine a lion tamer holding a stool facing my

My List of 100 Word Pictures

1. Tee	33. Mom	67. Check
2. Noah	34. Mare	68. Chef
3. Mow	35. Mail	69. Chop
4. Row	36. Match	70. Cozy
5. Lei	37. Mike	71. Cat
6. Jay	38. Muff	72. Cane
7. Key	39. Mob	73. Comb
8. Fee	40. Race	74. Car
9. Bee	41. Rat	75. Coal
10. Toes	42. Rain	76. Cash
11. Tot	43. Rum	77. Cake
12. Tin	44. Rear	78. Cough
13. Tame	45. Rail	79. Cap
14. Tire	46. Rash	80. Face
15. Tell	47. Rake	81. Fat
16. Tissue	48. Reef	82. Fan
17. Tack	49. Rope	83. Fume
18. Taffy	50. Lice	84. Fire
19. Tub	51. Lot	85. Fall
20. Nose	52. Lane	86. Fish
21. Net	53. Loom	87. Fang
22. Neon	54. Lair	88. Fife
23. Name	55. Lily	89. Fob
24. Nero	56. Lash	90. Base
25. Nail	57. Lick	91. Bat
26. Niche	58. Leaf	92. Bone
27. Neck	59. Lap	93. Bomb
28. Navy	60. Chase	94. Bar
29. Nap	61. Cheat	95. Bell
30. Mass	62. Chain	96. Bush
31. Mat	63. Chime	97. Bike
32. Mine	64. Chair	98. Buff
	65. Chile	99. Babe
	66. Judge	100. Thesis

boss since my word picture for 13 is tame (a lion tamer). If item 15 was a television set, I imagine William Tell shooting an arrow at a TV set on someone's head. If item 18 was a dish, I imagine taffy overflowing a kitchen dish or a satellite dish, whatever the picture in my mind.

When I started learning about remembering lists, I carried the list of sounds 0 to 9 in my pocket. Then I carried a list of the one hundred master words in my pocket. I asked people in my office to give me lists of one hundred items in any order. Then I asked them to question me randomly using any item on the list. I was able to accurately recall all hundred items within fifteen minutes. They were amazed and convinced that I had a great memory. They did not realize it was all in the system. You, the reader, can learn the system just as I did and master the memorization of lists.

If you want to remember a random list of ten thousand things (doesn't everybody?) just prepare a second list of one hundred picture words that match up to the master list. Two lists of one hundred picture words, side by side, allows you to remember ten thousand items. Start the second list with 00 for the word "sauce," and then expand the second list from 01 to 99. Tee is number 1 on the master list, so 01 on the second list could be golf course; 2 on the master list is Noah, so 02 on the second list could be boat; 3 on the master list is mow, so 03 on the second list could be clippers, and so on.

Now, let's assume someone gives you a list of ten thousand things to remember and number 1302 on the list is pancake. You would combine a picture of 13 on the master list (tame) and a picture of 02 from the second list, which is boat. So the picture in your mind would be a lion tamer on a boat taming a giant pancake. In a like manner, if you wanted to remember 8191 you would combine the picture of 81 on the master list, which is fat, and 91 on the second list, which is a baseball (derived from 91 on the master list, which is a bat). Those two pictures, fat and baseball, must be linked to 8191 on the list presented to you. For example, if 8191 is a book, just remember a very fat guy hitting a baseball after reading a book on how to hit.

It is a little complicated, but that's how you can remember ten thousand things in any order. The important idea to carry with you is that systems are the key to doing remarkable things—systems in mnemonics, math, reading, and in almost everything that you do.

Remembering one hundred things in any order is not just an academic exercise. It has numerous applications in everyday life. Here are just a few examples of what you might need to remember:

> 20 things to buy at a supermarket
>
> 8 errands to run
>
> 7 jokes you heard
>
> a number of answers to questions on a test
>
> travel directions
>
> vacation memories

The first two applications shown above are apparent; just connect the pictures in the master list to the items to buy in a supermarket or the destinations of errands. The third one, remembering jokes, is a little more difficult to accomplish. I just remember the key word in the punch line of the seven jokes and connect a picture of the key words with numbers one to seven of the master list. The use of the one hundred master words in tests is evident in cases where multiple reasons or attributes are required in answers.

Travel directions contain streets or highways. Streets are often named after trees, objects, or people. Highway numbers can be converted into words just as it was done in creating the master list. Highway 33 could be summarized in the word "mom." On a vacation you may have seen or done a number of things that you want to relate to your family or friends later on. This can easily be done by relating key words of the activities or sights to the master list.

Once you start applying mnemonic techniques, you may be surprised at the many useful ways you can remember things. An example in my experience happened two years ago when my wife and I rented a storage locker. A combination lock with four digits was used. I did not remember the combination, but I did remember that the first two digits added up to 7 and the second two digits also added up to seven and was a number approximately twice as large as the first two digits combined. Two years after renting the storage space my wife asked me to retrieve something, but we could not find the combination number for the lock. I went to the locker and tried 1 and 6, and then 3 and 4, and the lock opened.

Another time my wife and I wanted to buy some furniture at a Levitz store. We looked at many pieces of furniture and finally went to a salesman to take our order. I told the salesman the two pieces we were interested in and he said, "Thank you. I will go to those pieces of furniture and get the item numbers." I said, "No need to do that," and gave him, off the top of my head, the two ten-digit codes that were a combination of numbers and letters. He looked at me in amazement and said, "No one has ever done that before."

I was able to do these small feats of memory because random numbers can often be associated with things in the inner recesses of my memory, such as old home addresses, passwords, phone numbers, etc. If at one time I lived at a 416 address that number would still be ingrained in my memory. If I lived in apartment 23 in the past, I would remember that number. If there were a sequence of numbers that were all even, such as 246, I would remember that.

To aid in remembering a number like 85215, I would recall that the first four digits were descending and the fifth digit was the same as the second digit.

As for letters, I would convert them into numbers on the master list or make words out of them: "KP" for kitchen police, "LR" for left right, and so on. One time we ate at an outdoor seafood restaurant where food was ordered at an outside open window. There were eight people in our group. I took everyone's order and quickly added the number of like items, totaling, for example: 4 hamburgers, 6 French fries, 3 ears of corn, 6 lobster rolls, 4 iced teas, 2 soft drinks, and 2 diet soft drinks.

If you set your mind to remember something you may surprise yourself about how well you do. In my youth I would occasionally go to a dance. Sometimes I would ask the girl I was dancing with for her phone number. She would ask for a pencil and I would say no need for that, just tell me your phone number, I will remember it. The girl would be impressed and sometimes worry that I would not remember it, but I always did because the telephone number was of interest to me. If you are interested in something you are far more likely to remember it.

By the way, one of the tenets of a good memory is not to write things down. Once you write something down you almost surely will forget it. Your mind wipes it out of your data bank. If you are forced to memorize things you are likely not to forget them. It is like using a calculator to do simple math. By using a calculator to multiply simple numbers like 3×21 you are diminishing the ability to do math in your head. Memory is like a muscle that has to be used to retain its strength. There are people who may appear to be smarter than you. This may not be true. It may be that they have learned a systematic way of doing things, whether it is speed reading, doing math in their heads or memorizing things.

This book has given you a dozen or so pages on speed-reading, speed math, and mnemonics. Can you imagine how learned you would be if you had a full course on any of these subjects in high school, college, or adult education? I would wager that you would ace these subjects. It is never too late for you to take courses that will improve your ability to learn more and to learn faster. This book cannot teach you everything but it can open up new vistas of learning for you.

Chapter Seventeen

Speaking for Success

To rise in the ranks of corporations, clubs, or politics, it is important to learn how to speak with authority and sincerity. Whether speaking privately one-on-one or to a group of people, learning how to deliver thoughts and ideas succinctly and powerfully can help you succeed. I have given hundreds of speeches to groups ranging from fifty to fifteen hundred people in the United States and around the world, so I understand the challenge of entertaining and informing an audience. Public speaking comes easily to me because of attitude, training, and experience; I have also learned a great deal about how to make a powerful presentation. One must be knowledgeable about the subject, comfortable with the audience, and experienced in making presentations. Everyone can learn to be a good speaker with practice, courage, and confidence.

Learning to speak properly can start at home at an early age. For example, my wife and I had a lot of fun with our children while teaching them to make presentations. After dinner each of our three children was asked to give a two-minute speech to the family on a topic that we provided. The topics were simple, such as being asked to describe a pencil, a homework assignment, the New York Mets baseball team, or bugs in the garden. The two children listening to the talk had a great time criticizing their sibling with remarks like "she keeps moving her feet, she puts her hand to her face, she is looking down, she repeated herself," or "she said 'uh' too many times."

It was fun for everyone, yet serious. The children enjoyed critiquing each other and learned to be unafraid in front of a group. They absorbed the criticisms of their parents and siblings without rancor. Not only did the children learn to speak in front of a group; they learned to analyze the subject of their talk in real time to hone their skills. It prepared them for show-and-tell in school and for business meetings later in life. The US school system does not have much in the way of instruction in public speaking, but interchanges between students and teachers are a start. Colleges have debating societies that provide excellent forums for developing analytical capabilities and making public presentations.

It is amazing how many people who spoke to me intelligently and capably for fifteen or twenty minutes had later revealed to me their fear of speaking to an audience. It reminds me of people mentioned earlier in this book who said they had bad memories, yet could recall in minute detail events that happened decades ago.

To give a good speech, a certain level of confidence is required. Confidence is buttressed by a PowerPoint slide preparation, but please do not read the slides word for word because the audience has already read each one as soon as it appeared on the screen. Do not look away from the audience and at the screen behind you when discussing the material. Have a copy of the PowerPoint slides in front of you, and look at that as well as the audience. As you improve through experience you will learn to talk about the points rather than read the text on the slides.

For example, discuss the meaning of a graph and its implications rather than stating that X went from point A to point C and down to point D. At all times make sure that your voice projects loudly enough for everyone to hear. If there is a microphone available, use it effectively—better to be too loud than too soft. If you know your subject well and have given enough speeches on the topic, you will be able to speak without a written copy of the PowerPoint presentation. At that time, you may choose to write the points that you wish to make on a small piece of paper.

You can use mnemonics to remember the subjects so that notes are not even necessary. For example, if you have six points to make in your speech, these can be reduced to six words that you can make into a sentence; alternatively you can make an acronym of the first letter of key words in the six points.

I have seen many well-known people give poor speeches. Here is what they do wrong:

▷ They read their speech word for word instead of looking at the audience

▷ They fail to talk into the microphone

▷ They rush to get through too many PowerPoint slides

▷ They use type so small in their PowerPoint presentation that no one can read the small type

▷ They talk to the screen instead of the audience

▷ They talk well beyond the allotted time and throw off the entire meeting

▷ They start Q&A after they have spoken well beyond their allotted time

▷ They have a canned speech that is not appropriate for this particular audience

▷ They bore the audience

▷ Their answers to simple questions are exceedingly long

Now for the secrets of giving a great speech: First, know the subject, and be sure your knowledge is current. You do not have to be smarter than the audience on a particular subject because you may know one aspect better than the audience does. For example, I have spoken to PhDs in chemistry, health care, and computer science, and have zeroed in on my particular insights, such as connecting the topic with finance, taking a company public, or why outside expertise is necessary to augment their knowledge. I never write out a speech and never give the same speech twice. Every speech is extemporaneous.

I have broad, often even intimate, knowledge of the subject and offer original thought-provoking ideas. I immediately connect with the audience by making a humorous remark at the opening that gets everyone grinning and looking intently at me. I sprinkle my talk with humorous anecdotes and end with one as well. I do not use PowerPoint presentations because I want the audience looking at me instead of the screen. I would rather hand out PowerPoint material afterwards than have people looking at slides during the speech. I look to the left, the center, and to the right when talking to the audience.

When appropriate I use props to prove a point, as I did with a model car, which I move across the rostrum while stating that if car technology moved as fast as computer technology, a car could be driven from New York to San Francisco in hours instead of days. Another time I used a wedge of a three-inch diameter pie to show market share while commenting on increasing competition. Then I displayed a wedge of a ten-inch diameter pie illustrating that revenues will expand even as competition increases.

Hearing one speech after another at a conference makes for a long day. If it is time for your speech, a sprinkle of humor provides a welcome relief for the audience. You do not have to be a comedian to make the audience laugh. Some speakers have a knack of talking about ordinary things in a way that makes the audience chuckle. Sometimes you can engage the audience by asking them to raise their hands to answer a question.

A bond with the audience is one of the keys to making a good speech, which is why I enjoy having breakfast with the audience beforehand or meeting with them during breaks or lunch. After these informal get-togethers I feel more at ease with the audience and they with me. I also learn about their real interests, which I can refer to in my talk.

After a speech, attendees will come up to talk with you and exchange business cards. They may never contact you again, but be sure to look at the cards proffered and observe their names and organizations. Give attendees proper respect because they may become useful business or social contacts for you in the future.

Occasionally people who heard me speak twenty years ago have come up to me and recited my speech almost word for word because of the impact of the message and the emphasis provided by my props.

To those who need encouragement and confidence to speak in public, classes are offered in evening schools at adult education locations. One organization has been providing instruction on public speaking for over ninety years. Toastmasters International has more than 300,000 members in 14,650 clubs in well over one hundred countries. These clubs provide support, practice and awards to help members overcome their fears of public speaking. Annual membership fees are about $100. Many members enjoy the camaraderie and continue their membership for many years, some for twenty-five years or more. My advice to those who feel anguished speaking in public is to join Toastmasters International, make some friends and increase your skill.

While on the subject of public speaking, it would be good to give advice about audience behavior. Sometimes, at the end of a long talk, the speaker or moderator may say there is time for one quick question. Oblivious to the request for a quick question, someone goes on a three-minute-long rant and may not even get to a question. This is a killer for the audience. How many times have you been at a meeting when someone asks a question of the speaker that is not well thought out and apparently never-ending, forcing the speaker to cut the questioner off in the interest of time? There are several reasons for the never-ending question, including lack of cohesive thinking, desire to be heard and seen by others, and lack of knowledge about the subject.

Let's face it; there are a lot of long-winded people who are not cognizant of the clock and are unable to frame a cogent question. They seem oblivious of the desire of the audience to get to the next speaker, go to lunch, go home, or whatever. Make sure you are not one of them!

When you have an important interview for a job or membership in a club, you can use many of the techniques needed for giving a good speech. Look the interviewer in the eye, answer questions as thoroughly and succinctly as possible, and do not be afraid to say "I do not know the answer." Any salesman knows that the key rule in sales is to ask for the order, and when you get it stop talking and leave. There is always a chance that the offer will be withdrawn if you keep talking. For example, if you continue to talk it is possible that you will reveal a problem that will nullify the offer. Quit while you are ahead.

To prepare for an interview you should do what is called "due diligence." Research the company or organization you are meeting with, and, if possible, the interviewer as well. Look around the office or room where the interview takes place and observe pictures, artwork, or diplomas that you can refer to in conversation with the interviewer. Finding areas of common interest with the person interviewing you improves the atmosphere by making it friendlier. Turn off your mobile phone before the meeting. Organize answers for the questions you know will be asked and formulate the questions you need answered. Follow up the interview with a prompt and thoughtful thank you note.

Having an impact on an audience is one thing; making an impact on one person is something else. Let me give you a recent example. A friend wanted me to meet the CEO of an emerging technology company that was seeking funding. I waited at a restaurant for his arrival. When he approached, he shook my hand and introduced himself and his wife, who looked at me and said she knows me. This is not uncommon, as many people know me from speeches that I give, but this meeting with her seemed new to me. I said, "I am sorry, but I do not recall ever meeting you." Then she mentioned an investment-banking firm that I worked at four decades ago. Befuddled, I acknowledged she was correct.

She went on to relate an anecdote to me. As a young girl she worked with me at the investment banking firm, and one day she told me she felt she would be pretty for only three more years. I told her that this was a nonsensical thought; she would be pretty for the rest of her life. And here she was, as beautiful as ever forty-two years later, telling me of the positive effect I had on her life when I told her the simple truth.

Part 4

BE MORE PROSPEROUS

"Success is stumbling from failure to failure with no loss of enthusiasm."—WINSTON CHURCHILL

"The way to get started is to quit talking and begin doing."—WALT DISNEY

"The harder you work, the luckier you get."
—MICHAEL BLOOMBERG

Epiphany

I am a competitor. I wanted to excel in sports, be a better student, and do better than my coworkers. I practiced to be a better ballplayer, I read books to be a better student, and I worked harder than others to excel in business. I was the first one in and the last one to leave in all of my jobs. Working harder made up for any deficiencies in experience or background. I have never missed a day of sports, school, or work in my life. Dependability is the essence of success.

Chapter Eighteen

Common-Sense Savings

WRITING ABOUT BECOMING MORE PROSPEROUS is challenging because readers have a wide variety of attitudes and interests. Poor people want to become rich, rich people want to become millionaires, and millionaires want to become billionaires. It seems that no one is satisfied with their status; but that is not a bad thing. Desiring a better life for yourself and your family is a basic human instinct. Yearning to become financially secure can be realized through money, education, marriage, friendships, or hard work. If you are happy, healthy, and smart you have a leg up on a large segment of humanity. Becoming more prosperous is a challenge not easily met but readily achievable.

Before getting into esoteric subjects like macroeconomics and sophisticated investment instruments, let us start with something simple—common sense. People with addictions like alcoholism, smoking, gambling, and shopping are always racing up the down escalators. Eventually those with these addictions need to seek help because the escalator is not taking them to their desired destination—happiness and financial security. Let us briefly review these five addictions: alcohol, drugs, smoking, gambling, and spending (credit card abuse).

Alcoholism is a serious illness. Drinking to excess can eventually cause death through liver disease, but can also ruin lives in many other ways. Binge drinking destroys brain cells affecting memory and balance. Moreover, excess drinking inevitably leads to an unhealthy diet that further adversely affects the brain. We have all seen drunks that can barely stand up and are often agitated, angry, and confused.

Fortunately, before ruining their health, marriage, family, and finances, alcoholics have recourse. Alcoholics Anonymous is a highly regarded nationwide organization with locations in major cities throughout the world. At these centers people suffering from alcoholism are anonymously accepted into groups coping with the same problem. Under the guidance of a leader, members talk about their struggles with alcoholism and how they put their lives back together again.

Some continue to go to meetings even after having kicked the habit twenty or thirty years ago. Hearing from others with the same addiction helps new members cope with their own addictions. By ceasing to drink, alcoholics will save money and be happier, healthier, smarter, and richer in more ways than can be imagined.

Drugs are the most serious addiction, starting with prescriptions for pain killers and the like and escalating to marijuana, cocaine, heroin, and various narcotic mixes. Drug addiction afflicts all classes and social levels, including the rich, the famous, and the poor. An increasing number of drug addicts, whether elderly or adolescent, succumb to drug overdoses and die. Entertainers are especially prone to drugs because of peer pressure and the stress of performing in front of live audiences. Youngsters are introduced to drugs by their families, classmates, and friends.

Most drugs are grown or manufactured abroad and smuggled into the United States at alarming rates. Illegal drugs are a huge international business and almost impossible to stop despite presidential campaigns like "Just Say No" and the efforts of U.S. Immigration and Customs Enforcement of laws to combat illegal narcotics. Nationally, the Drug Enforcement Agency (DEA) cooperates with state and local police agencies to counter drug trafficking and drug use.

Practically all states have an office of alcoholism and substance abuse, but their services have failed to mitigate the problem in any major way. There are also numerous local charitable institutions addressing the problems of addiction, such as the New York Center for Living, which offers adolescents and young adults outpatient treatment for alcohol and substance abuse. Families of the patients are included as part of the solution. If you or someone you know has a drug problem, a local group is probably available to help alleviate the problem.

Smoking is more costly than ever, and the habit is almost certain to kill you if you live long enough and are fortunate enough to avoid other deadly diseases. If you still smoke despite ubiquitous anti-smoking advertising and the increasing stigma associated with smoking, you need help. E-cigarettes may be an answer, but it is too early to tell. Regulation by the Federal Government is a certainty.

Smokers should seek counseling from local support groups or the American Lung Association, both of which offer smoking cessation classes, morale support, and the provision of drugs and nicotine patches to wean smokers away from their addiction. The American Lung Association has established a Freedom from Smoking online support group for computer users. By ceasing to smoke, cigarette users, like alcoholics, will also save money and be happier, healthier, smarter, and richer in more ways than can be imagined.

Gambling is an addiction that is growing rapidly because barriers to gambling are coming down due to the needs of municipalities to increase revenues. Many years ago, legal gambling in the United States was restricted to horseracing. Then casino gambling took root, first in Las Vegas, then in Atlantic City, and thereafter on numerous Indian Reservations. Now gambling is available on the Internet. The trend is clearly in the direction of more legalized gambling. Illegal gambling with local bookmakers (bookies) has been around for centuries.

In the future, legalized gambling will probably be allowed for sporting events, which is already offered in Las Vegas. It is one thing to travel to a destination city to gamble; it is another to be able to gamble from the comfort of one's home by telephone, computer, or mobile device.

The pernicious habit of gambling is going to ruin many more lives in the future than most people realize. Gamblers Anonymous is a fast growing organization tailored along the lines of Alcoholics Anonymous and is the place to go to get help. Like the other addictions, ceasing to gamble recklessly will save you money and make you happier, healthier, smarter, and richer in more ways than can be imagined.

Another addiction abetted by the proliferation of credit cards is the unfettered ability to spend without the ability to repay. Credit cards enable ordinary people to become shopaholics. Mentally, it is much easier to make purchases with a credit card than to actually hand over cash.

Both the United States government and American families as a whole have the highest levels of debt in US history. In the spring of 2015 politicians decried the fact that the total public debt outstanding was a record $18.6 trillion. What you do not hear much about is that American consumers owe $11.9 trillion in personal debt, 70 percent of which is in the form of mortgages and the remainder is from credit card debt and student loans.

College students have borrowed heavily through the Federal Student Loan Program to finance their education. Many of those debts are in default because of an inability by former students to find jobs that will enable them to pay down the debt.

The overall family debt burden, including money owed for mortgages, auto and college loans, and credit card purchases, is making it difficult for families to stay solvent.

Exacerbating the situation are the exorbitant interest fees charged by credit card companies for late payments. I know wealthy people who are paying 18 percent credit card fees and are too ignorant to pay their credit card fees down with money they could borrow at 4 percent. It used to be that poor people were the only ones paying ultra-high interest rates on purchases, but now even high-paid executives are falling into the trap.

Come to your senses people! Either pay cash for purchases or pay your credit card bills in full and on time. Do not buy beyond your means, and do not carry credit card charges month to month. By not overspending and by paying bills on time, you will save money and be happier, healthier, smarter, and richer in more ways than can be imagined.

Of the addictive vices covered here, gambling, drugs, and borrowing are on the ascension, while smoking and drinking are in decline. As Shakespeare counseled in *Hamlet,* "neither a borrower nor a lender be." This famous Shakespeare quotation applies to personal relationships, not business relationships. It is perfectly fine for corporations to issue bonds. On the personal side of things, I have learned from experience that whenever I lend money, books, or tools there is a good chance I will not have them repaid or returned in a timely fashion, if at all.

There are lots of ways to save money for those on tight budgets: eating in instead of out, watching movies at home instead of going to the theatre, and collecting coupons and shopping wisely. Recently, there was a lady in front of me at a supermarket checkout counter. Her bill was about $150 and she paid the entire amount with coupons. I was delayed, but not disturbed by the ringing up of her many purchases and the scanning of her numerous coupons. Instead, I was intrigued by her ability to fill up a shopping cart with food and sundries and not have to pay anything at all.

I talked with the checkout clerk and learned that this woman used coupons from numerous sources that included store fliers, checkout coupons, manufacturer's coupons, online coupons, and the customer discount card issued by the store. I am sure that it took quite a bit of time for the sophisticated shopper to accumulate all the coupons, but like any job, she thought it was worth her time to obtain discounted merchandise.

No matter how rich one is, everyone likes to get a good deal. I can afford to pay top prices and buy whatever I need, but I employ sensible strategies that save money and are also fun. I present a supermarket card to the checkout person, and everything on sale is automatically given to me at the sale price. I buy things with long expiration dates like toothpaste, shaving cream, drinks, and cookies only when they go on sale. Why would I pay five dollars for an item when I can get it for three dollars on sale a week or two later. J.P. Morgan famously said: "If you have to ask how much something costs, you cannot afford it." Well, I am not J.P. Morgan, but a Depression-era baby, raised on frugality.

We have a summer home, so we pay monthly for basic services such as electric, gas, water, telephone, TV, and Internet in two places. However, we suspend all of the services at the summer home for six months in the winter when not living there. Many other people with vacation homes neglect to suspend their services and pay hundreds of dollars a month for nothing.

Families often bemoan the fact that their money is rapidly depleting for no apparent reason. They ignore certain facts. For example, the annual cost of owning a car escalated sharply until gas prices plunged early in 2015. If a car is driven 15,000 miles a year and gets 15 mpg, it burns 1,000 gallons of gasoline. At a price of three dollars per gallon, the annual fuel cost is $3,000, and on top of that is the cost of maintenance and tolls. The family next door may have purchased a car that gets 30 mpg and pays $1,500 or half as much per year for fuel.

In an analogy from the business world, when a company strives to increase revenues by 10 percent, only 1 or 2 percent of the 10 percent increase drops to the bottom line because of expenses and taxes. In contrast, cutting costs by 10 percent increases the bottom line by a full 10 percent. The lesson is that cutting costs, not increasing income, is the way to salvage your budget. In high-tax states, high earners would have to earn $6,000 to pay for $3,000 of gasoline purchases. Reducing costs offsets the need for higher pre-tax earnings. As Benjamin Franklin said: "A penny saved is a penny earned."

The world is full of people who live beyond their means. Laid-off executives who never had to budget helplessly watch their savings disappear. Professional football players earning huge salaries are often bankrupt within three years of retiring. The perils of affluence are often recognized too late. Get-rich-quick investors exalt when their stocks rise but have no backup plan when their stocks plummet. A conservative approach to investing and living will produce less stress and better sleep.

Chapter Nineteen

Getting the Right Job

IN TIMES OF ECONOMIC MALAISE, unemployment rises to the point where discouragement sets in; people stop looking for work and are no longer categorized as unemployed. The period from 2010 to 2015 is such a time. The social safety net in Europe and the United States has managed to keep people and families afloat. The great majority of people would like to earn an honest living but cannot find meaningful employment. The situation is getting worse despite popular online venues such as ZipRecruiter, Beyond, LinkedIn, and Monster, which can help people seeking employment. Years ago newspaper want ads were the way to find a job. Now, newspaper circulation and classified ads are in serious decline. People prefer to do their tasks online. Classified ads have migrated to websites such as Craigslist and Angie's List. Old ways of obtaining jobs are out and new ways are in.

The rapid advance of technology is eliminating some jobs and creating others. The service industry is growing while the manufacturing industry is declining. Many old skills are no longer needed while newer skills are in short supply. Once secretaries had to know stenography, but now bosses type their own emails. Switchboard operators have become obsolete due to automation. Assembly-line workers are being replaced by sophisticated robots. Tollbooth collectors are becoming a rarity, replaced by automated tollbooths. Teachers are losing out to online courses given to thousands, if not hundreds of thousands of people. Times are changing, so if you want a new or more permanent job, get with it and learn new skills.

I have a theory I will call the "C Theory" that has helped me personally. Hold your right hand in front of you in the shape of a backward C with your thumb at the bottom. Hold up your left hand in the shape of a C with the fingers of your left hand above the fingers of your right hand. The theory is that if the salary range in your current occupation is from, let us say, $75,000 at the right thumb level and $150,000 at the right finger level, and you are moving up the salary ladder, when you get midway to the top of the salary range, it is the time to consider moving to another job where the salary at the left thumb level is at the bottom of a new pay scale, say from $100,000 to $200,000.

"C Theory" — Salary Range

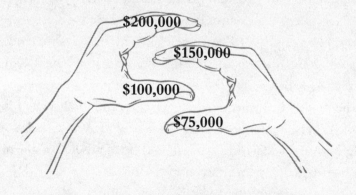

Many years ago when the computer industry was just beginning, I took a college course on the Univac 1 computer which I learned to program in COBOL. That single course changed my career trajectory. I took my first computer job with Univac at a lower salary, but quickly rose to a much higher salary level than my old job would have permitted. With the "C Theory" I skipped from the right hand range to the left hand range and back to the right hand range, and so on, to attain better jobs with higher salaries. Greater knowledge should ultimately lead to greater income. As an aside, even today I continue to take adult education courses to keep current and for amusement.

Many immigrants work at two jobs to pay the rent and feed the family. Two jobs can be better than one because eventually you can choose to spend more time in the better job. I have talked to dozens of people who were unhappy in their job and wanted to leave. Some of those people started moonlighting in a second job that eventually became their primary job. Many had menial jobs that gave them an opportunity to use their pleasing personalities. Their jobs were as doormen, elevator starters, and hatcheck girls, which entailed daily contact with high-level business people. This enabled them to initiate conversations with selected tenants or customers who could help them land a better job.

Be alert to casual contacts with people who can help you. If you are out of work, or unhappy in your job, discretely mention this to your friends who can help you secure new employment. Use your Facebook page or LinkedIn site in a professional manner to tell people about your availability, but do not be antagonistic about your present or past employer. Membership in a club or group can expand your social network in a very personal way. Use those relationships to further your career.

Executive search firms and employment agencies can also be useful. You have nothing to lose by going to one. Even if they do not have an immediate job available, they will render useful advice. You need a good resume, and one page is best. Busy people would prefer to read one page. If your range of skills and experience is long and varied, you should prepare a specialized resume for each employment opportunity. Most of the resume can be the same for each interview as far as your education, hobbies, and awards, but your work experience should be tailored to meet the specific requirements of the targeted job.

Do not be embarrassed about disclosing your situation and seeking help, because even the most talented and experienced people require assistance. For example, executives want to serve on boards of directors or obtain executive positions in emerging or stable companies. Alternatively, many college students will work as interns for little or no salary in the summer to enhance their resume or learn about a business. This often leads to permanent employment.

Entrepreneurship and venture capital seem to be the buzz right now because of the proliferation of young people and college dropouts that have started online enterprises which have achieved valuations in the millions or even billions of dollars. Founders and early employees of these companies have become very rich. Just look through magazines like *Forbes*, *Fortune*, and *Business Week* to read case histories of those who have started successful businesses. If they can do it, maybe you can too. If you do not subscribe to these magazines, they are available free at public libraries and on the web.

I have personally experienced this phenomenon, since my firm has been the first venture capital investor in ten companies that have gone on to be worth over $1 billion, and up to $75 billion in one case. If you are yearning to start a company, take your chances today and become the business scion of tomorrow.

Chapter Twenty

Beating Inflation

TO MAKE INVESTMENTS you need money, and to have money you need income, or at least a good job or savings. Proceeds from investments should exceed the negative effects of inflation and transaction costs. The value of a dollar changes every day from the forces of inflation, production, and monetary policy. Your net worth and cash are diminished when income does not keep pace with rising prices for housing, travel, clothing, food, entertainment, and just about everything else. If your income is not rising as fast as the rate of inflation you are losing purchasing power. Conservative investors may have all their money in very safe bank savings accounts or municipal bonds earning, let's say, 1 percent a year, but their financial situation is deteriorating because inflation is rising at a rate faster than 2 percent annually. The goal is to maintain net worth or have income in excess of the rate of inflation.

Inflation affects people in different ways. People who own expensive homes may experience a huge increase in their net worth when home prices rise, but people renting apartments are losing out to inflation. The rising costs of heating oil, gasoline, food, and clothing have to be offset by higher wages or investment gains. When interest rates are low, retirees on fixed income are especially hard hit because they rely on income from social security and savings accounts.

There are many paths to prosperity, and which path you take is an individual choice. Even without investments you can become wealthy by starting a company, being an early employee in a hot company, or by climbing the corporate ladder of an established company. The quickest way to riches is through owning stock, stock options, or getting large bonuses. Others become rich by starting small companies or by saving money and investing wisely. Some are fortunate enough to have inherited their wealth. The wise expand their wealth by making the right decisions, hiring the right people, and investing intelligently. Alternatively, some of the wealthy lose it all on bad decisions, vices, addictions, or get-rich schemes. I have seen it all.

I have worked in menial jobs, and I have run companies. I have worked on Wall Street and in industry. I have advised independent investors, the largest pension funds in the world, and both small and large corporations on how to successfully manage their money. Before reaching my teens I pushed an ice cream cart to earn a few dollars, and I also helped assemble the first ballpoint pens. I have run a hedge fund, taken my own company public, and advised ten of the largest companies in the world while managing their money in venture capital funds. The lessons I have learned from these experiences I want to pass on to you.

People work hard to earn money, but that is only half of the battle. The other half involves saving money and investing wisely to build up a nest egg for an enjoyable retirement and old age. I have seen many people blow their money on having a good time and on penny stock investments that almost never work out. The key to being a successful investor is to depend on the advice and experience of licensed professionals who manage investment funds or who are registered to provide advice. Family offices, pension funds, and family endowments make sophisticated investments in hedge funds that invest in stocks or bonds and also in alternative investments, such as venture capital, and timber, oil, and gas partnerships.

Corporations frequently offer 401K plans or Roth IRAs to their employees. Those accounts are managed by sophisticated money managers. In many ways a Roth IRA is an improvement over the typical 401K plan because gains on the investments are not taxed upon withdrawal but are taxed at the onset. So, if you have investments that you believe are going to increase greatly in value, you would be better off tax-wise having a Roth IRA. I would not advise people to invest in individual stocks until they gain experience or have studied and understand accounting, economics, and financial statements.

An analysis of investment returns is tricky because it all depends on the starting and closing dates. The oldest expression on Wall Street is "buy low, sell high." It is easy to say, but hard to do. You are just as likely to come in at the top of the cycle as the bottom of the cycle. In fact, history shows that more people come in at the top because of unbounded optimism and a follow-the-herd mentality. One technique to avoid the ups and downs is called "dollar cost averaging." This is where you invest the same amount on a regular basis (say $500 per month) and in weak markets obtain more shares than normal. This is called averaging down or "dollar cost averaging."

Average annual returns on an investment in the S&P 500 stock index from 1928 to 2013 have been a whopping 11.5 percent. From 2004 to 2013 the average return was 9.1 percent. There are numerous studies on average returns in the stock market and on bonds, but I caution that it all depends on the starting and ending point. A conservative rule of thumb is that stocks in the long-term return 7.5 percent annually, and bonds earn 3.5 percent.

With this in mind, most advisors recommend a mix of stocks and bonds with about 2/3rds in stocks and 1/3rd in bonds. Bonds offer a steady income from interest payments, and there is a wide choice of bonds ranging from stable to risky (junk bonds), from taxable to nontaxable (municipal bonds), and, finally, corporate bonds. Stocks, like bonds, also offer a steady stream of income in the form of dividends. Most large companies pay dividends while smaller companies do not, as they instead use their funds to invest in growth. Investments in bonds and stocks are never absolutely safe. Prices of bonds and stocks can go down or up, and bankruptcies are always a possibility.

The idea of investments for individuals is not to make a fortune, but to make a good return on investments and stay ahead of inflation. Investors who believe they can beat the market are delusional, because even most professionals cannot beat the overall market on a consistent basis. There are transaction costs for purchasing and selling, which can be quite high if the account is turned over frequently (churned). Be wary of mutual funds that have high costs for initial investors known as front-end loaded. It can take a year or two just to break even.

Chapter Twenty-One

Five Insights on Life and Business

WISDOM GLEANED OVER THE YEARS from people I know or admire has provided me with guidance, buttressed my philosophy of life, and helped me in business. Read on. Here are some thoughts on my favorite insights, including the last that is the key to being more prosperous.

INSIGHT #1

"If a problem has no solution, it may not be a problem, but is rather a fact—not to be solved, but to be coped with over time."

I had the honor of introducing Shimon Peres, the ninth president of Israel, at a conference in Israel in 1998. This was just after Dame Margaret Thatcher and I, among several others, received the 50th Anniversary Israel Award. Shimon Peres talked to me before his presentation and gave me some words of wisdom that I reflect in insight #1. His insight rang true to me because I know people who have been stymied trying to find a solution for a fact. Problems may be based on facts, but facts in themselves cannot be changed. There is no solution for a fact. Other people have told me about real problems, not facts of life, for which I could offer reasonable solutions that did not occur to them.

My advice is always to focus on solutions rather than problems. Too often people are unable to solve their problems because they are ill, depressed, confused, and they cannot think straight. Many times I feel I was put on Earth to help other people solve problems because I am always thinking clearly. Thanks to Simon Peres I frequently tell people with a so-called problem that it cannot be solved because they are dealing with a fact of life and not a problem.

INSIGHT #2

"At IBM, the idea is not to make the right decision; it is to make the decision right."

When I worked in Wall Street I followed IBM very closely and was often quoted in newspapers and magazines when IBM made news or reported financial results. I got to know many of the distinguished IBM CEOs, the first of whom was Vincent Learson. One time I spoke with him on the telephone, and he gave me this insight on how IBM continued to be a highly successful company. I have seen this quote attributed to numerous people, but to my mind, it came first from Vincent Learson, and it was included in a book he wrote about IBM.

His insight is important and may account for one of the reasons I am always happy. I know people who second-guess themselves immediately after making a decision. They drive to an event and on the way complain about having chosen to attend it, or they choose a restaurant and complain that they should have gone to a different restaurant, and so on. Once you make a decision, live with it and make it right. If the decision turns out to be bad, make another decision, but don't look back, only forward. It is a waste of time and energy to complain—either act or acquiesce.

INSIGHT #3

"Work expands so as to fill the time available for its completion."

This valuable insight comes from *Parkinson's Law,* a book written by C. Northcote Parkinson in 1957. It is a great book about management, and the anecdotes in it are very humorous. *Parkinson's Law* has become famous. Last year in a used bookstore in Boothbay Harbor, Maine, I found a book of proverbs that I purchased for two dollars. To my amazement, amidst all the proverbs from olden times was *Parkinson's Law.*

I know people who, when they have a speech to give three months hence, spend a great deal of time gathering clippings and thinking about the speech almost every day. I am a strong proponent of *Parkinson's Law,* which guides me in my activities. It may be hard to believe, but if I am giving a speech three months from now I do not think of it until I arrive at the venue. I am usually very familiar with the subject and am comfortable giving presentations, so why worry about the speech. I will have read newspapers and magazines and watched TV during the three-month period, and what I have learned becomes part of my speech.

I speak to the audience the way I would speak to an individual. I relate the content to the interests of the audience and make predictions about the future from what I have learned from the past to the present. Speakers can be too well prepared, thereby losing spontaneity in their presentations. Some may feel this is blasphemy. However, I think over preparation is just as injurious as being under-prepared.

INSIGHT #4

"Collect the facts; Analyze the facts; Decide. (CAD)"

People like to jump to conclusions earlier than they should. For example, a high school student applied for admission to six colleges. She was accepted at three and had not heard from the other three, yet she was spending time and effort talking to me about which college to attend. She asked my advice, and I replied that I could not offer advice because all the facts were not in. I gave her my personal insight, "CAD." I said that I could not offer an opinion until after she heard from the other colleges. The expression "jumping to conclusions" is apt. As a researcher and securities analyst I appreciate the value of collecting all the facts before making a decision, or else the decision could be erroneous.

INSIGHT #5

"Buy the haystack instead of the needle."

When it comes to epiphanies, John Bogle, founder of The Vanguard Mutual Fund Company, had a whopper of an insight when it came to buying stocks, which he put into action—thereby creating a huge industry. John Bogle did a statistical analysis that showed that stock market indices almost always outperformed the results of active money managers with their high fees and extensive transaction costs. Moreover, the stellar results of the best fund managers are an integral part of the indices. The biggest index of all is the S&P 500, which accounts for approximately 73 percent of the value of all US stocks.

John Bogle realized that individual investors would achieve higher returns by buying a very low cost index of all stocks rather than by buying a high-risk portfolio of only a few stocks. John Bogle went on to write a dozen books on investments. His idea of an index fund was ridiculed by many, but index funds have become a huge industry and propelled Vanguard into the largest mutual fund organization in the world. Index funds can be purchased as Exchange Traded Funds "ETFs" or as mutual funds. I was proud to visit with John (Jack) Bogle at the headquarters of Vanguard late in 2014.

I worked at Drexel Burnham in the 1970s when Michael Milken, much like John Bogle, had a simple idea that built an industry. The insight from his original idea had to do with bonds. He too did a statistical analysis, which showed bonds of small companies, derogatorily named "junk bonds," did not suffer defaults much more than those of larger companies, but, importantly, the interest rates for junk bonds were much higher than for bonds of larger companies. From that insight, a concept developed that enabled Drexel Burnham to become a major investment-banking firm rivaling its larger, more established peers. All of the largest investment banking firms eventually entered the junk bond market.

In recent years, entrepreneurs have had insights that have led to fabulously successful companies such as Facebook, LinkedIn, eBay, YouTube, Alibaba, Uber and Airbnb. Funding to fuel the growth of these and other companies have come from venture capital and

Wall Street. You may not have an insight to build a company as big as Google or Amazon, but you never know. New companies are started every day. Acting upon an idea by obtaining funding and starting a company takes guts, not to mention perseverance and burning desire.

Everyone has insights. They are likely not as big as those of Henry Ford or Thomas Edison, but they are insights nonetheless. If you want to get ahead, insights are invaluable.

Chapter Twenty-Two

Gambling Is Not Investing

YOUR CHANCES OF BEING a successful investor are all in the odds. Imagine that you belong to a club or any large group of people and ask each of them to flip a coin 50 times. The winner would be the one whose coin came up heads the most times. We all know that on average there will be 25 heads and 25 tails but someone, by the laws of chance, will have the highest number of heads, perhaps 35. That person will be the winner and may even boast about his ability to obtain the desired result, heads. The same is true in the world of investing; there are always random winners and losers. But the real winners are those that win consistently year after year by demonstrating ability rather than chance. The difference between coin tossing and investing is that professional investors, through intelligence, analysis, timing, and due diligence shift the odds of winning in their favor.

The performance of money managers is available for all to see; it is audited and overseen by the SEC, FINRA, and state regulators. The problem in seeking high-level performance is that some money managers do better than others in up markets, but worse in down markets, and some do well in inflationary times and others in deflationary times, and so forth.

Some may not know that they have someone managing their money if their company invests their IRA through one or more money managers that are invisible to the employee. Other people deal with brokers who give advice and may also have discretion to manage their funds.

How do we measure success or failure in this? A benchmark is necessary. In public stocks the benchmark is most commonly the S&P 500 Index, but there are numerous other indices representing segments of the market. The simple truth is that in a great many cases, active money managers do not outperform the S&P 500 over the long term because of management fees and brokerage fees for buying and selling stocks. There is a way to achieve stock market success which I will describe a little later, but will first give a primer on odds (percentages).

Organizations that run the stock exchanges, casinos, race tracks, lotteries, and raffles all enjoy "the take." What does that mean? It means that the establishment (sometimes called the House) takes a portion of what is invested or gambled. "The take" also known as the takeout, the commission, or the vigorish, is shown in the following table.

Approximate Takeouts	
Raffle	50–80%
Lottery	30–50%
Horseracing	15–25%
Sports betting	5–10%
Slots	5–10%
Casino	1–5%
Stock/bond trades	0–2%

People know they are being ripped off in raffles and lotteries, but they accept it because of the hype about "Hey, somebody has to win," and the money usually goes to good causes such as local philanthropies or education. "The takeout" on sports betting is lower than for raffles or lotteries, but bettors can become addicted and lose in the long run because of "the take." Horserace and sports betters are especially addictive because they watch events in person or on television and enjoy matching wits with the House.

Imagine a friendly card game of poker with five players. The host offers his living room with a card table and lots of food for the players. All he asks is five dollars from every pot. If the game goes on for a long time, guess who ends up with all the money? Well, the host of course, because of "the take."

When a charity holds a raffle, it may take as much as 80 percent of the proceeds for itself and give out prizes amounting to only 20 percent of the proceeds. A typical prize could be a $35,000 automobile for $100,000 in proceeds. The car is usually donated, so the charity might be ahead by $100,000, not $65,000. People buying raffle tickets do not mind being on the losing end of the odds if it is for a good cause.

In lotteries conducted by states, the winning pool can be in the hundreds of millions of dollars, particularly if there was no winner the previous week. Depending on the state in which lottery tickets are sold, between 33 percent and 50 percent of the proceeds are taken out before distributions to the winners who must pay taxes on winnings.

Horse racing has been around for a long time. People like to bet on the horses at county fairs or at fancy racetracks. Admission fees are low because the track makes money on pari-mutuel betting where computers instantly reflect odds and payoffs for win, place, and show for the top three horses and for more exotic bets as well.

Winning horses receive purses generally ranging from $1,000 to $1,000,000 depending on the caliber of horses. Approximately 20 percent of money wagered is kept by the track for purses, maintenance, and the safety of the horses. The actual take is 15–20 percent on simple bets, such as win place and show, and about 25 percent on exotic bets involving selecting two or more horses in daily doubles, exactas, and trifectas.

In a gambling casino there are different games to play, including 21, roulette, and craps. The card game 21 requires some skill, such as remembering cards that have been played. Craps does not really require skill except in making smart bets, such as pass or don't pass, that have a low takeout versus foolish bets that have a very high takeout. Many of the bets in craps can be almost even money; if you stick to those bets you can gamble at the craps table a long time and have a decent chance of winning.

Roulette is pure chance, but some bets are worse than others; you can bet on a single number at long odds or you can bet on red/black or even/odd at short odds. If you bet on roulette, "the takeout" is about 5 percent, so if you play for a long time you will probably lose money. If you play the slot machines for a long period of time the odds are that you will lose because the takeout is 5–10 percent.

Betting on sporting events is forbidden everywhere in the United States except Las Vegas. The House take, called vigorish on sports bets, is generally 9 percent. For example, you have to bet eleven dollars to win ten dollars on a game that is considered even or made even by giving or taking points or runs. Illegal gambling with local bookies is available in every major city.

There is a well-known expression that "the House always wins," the House being the racetrack, gambling casino, raffler, state lottery commission, or bookie. Wouldn't it be nice to be the House and not the sucker. The House takes out a commission on all the money gambled by winners and losers so the House always wins. There is a difference between investing and gambling. If you invest wisely, as opposed to gambling on games of chance, you can in effect be the House. As an investor the odds can be with you instead of against you.

Chapter Twenty-Three

May the Odds Be with You

As DEMONSTRATED, IN GAMBLING AND lotteries the odds always favor the House because of "the takeout," so the House never loses. You can, in effect, be the House if you invest wisely for the long term. A long history spanning one hundred years of positive statistical results is the equivalent of "the takeout" when it comes to investments. If you follow the advice in this book you will almost certainly be a successful investor because the odds are greatly in your favor. If you bet on the horses or at a gambling casino it is always possible that you will be a winner for a day—but not in the long term. If you gamble steadily you will surely lose money. In investing, the opposite is true; if you invest wisely you will be a winner in the long term but not necessarily in the short term.

There are three fundamental concepts necessary to understand how to be a successful investor.

> **Dollar Cost Averaging** involves making steady investments regardless of rises or declines in stock prices or interest rates. If you are investing $1,000 a month in a particular stock, you will get more shares when the stock price declines and fewer shares when the stock price rises.

Compound Interest is earning interest on interest or dividends on dividends. Investments or savings grow rapidly because of compounding.

Index Funds are a way to match the performance of a large group of stocks instead of attempting to beat the market by investing in individual companies. It is simply just buying and holding stocks without doing research. Stocks are purchased in proportion to their relative market value or stock price. Costs for this method of investing are extremely low. It has been shown that low costs are the best indicator of good performance.

Let's start off by discussing dollar cost averaging. To invest you need money. Money can come from savings, marrying well or benefiting from a bequest. If you are in the habit of saving money in a bank account or certificate of deposit, the money will appreciate surprisingly fast. There is the law of 72. This law describes how long it takes to double your money at various growth or interest rates. Just divide the magic number 72 by the growth rate and you will get the answer. If your money is growing at 36 percent a year, it will take only two years to double your money; at 10 percent it would take 7.2 years and at 5 percent doubling would occur in about 14 years. This may seem like a long time to you, but if you save money every month the money will add up quickly.

If your company offers an IRA in which a percentage of your salary is deposited in your account every year, you are ahead of the game. If the company allows you to match their IRA contribution, do it. IRA money is generally invested in the company stock or a choice of mutual funds.

The power of compound interest is a well-proven concept. It simply means earning interest on interest and not just on the principal. Benjamin Franklin, a Founding Father of the United States, was a brilliant statesman and scientist. He understood the value of compound interest when he created two trusts of $4,500: one for Boston and one for Philadelphia. After one hundred years, three-fourths of the funds were released to the respective cities and the remainder reinvested for another one hundred years. During these periods the principal was available to make loans to young people for apprenticeships at 5 percent interest. After the first one hundred years, approximately $500,000 was available to each city, and after the second one hundred years, Philadelphia received $2 million and Boston over $5.5 million.

There are dozens of money managers who have a long-term record of beating the averages, but there are hundreds who have mixed records. A recent study by S&P and Dow Jones titled "Does Past Performance Matter? The Persistence Scorecard," the performance of funds as reported by the *New York Times*, found that only 2 out of 2,862 Funds in the top quartile of performance managed to stay in the top quartile for four consecutive years.

Warren Buffett is famous for his strategy of buying stocks (or companies) at low valuations and holding them for a long time. Importantly, the buy and hold strategy limits transaction costs of frequent trading which eat away at profits. If you invest with any one of the relatively few proven investment managers like Warren Buffet, almost all require minimum investments ranging from $10,000 to $100,000 or more.

If you do not have the good fortune to be in a position to invest with a premier money manager, there is an alternative, which I heartily endorse. Invest in an index fund such as an S&P 500 fund whose component companies represent about 3/4 of the total US equity market. There are also index funds for the total market, small cap stocks, foreign stocks, technology, and other segments of the market for those seeking higher returns but with increased risk.

Approximately 70 percent of the money invested in index funds are in the S&P 500 index. Index funds were famously started in the early 1970s by John Bogle of Vanguard. The largest providers of index funds are Vanguard, BlackRock, Fidelity, and State Street.

Study after study has shown that index funds have superior performance compared to managed funds with their high fees. Of course, some money managers in any given year do better than index funds, but that is not so in the aggregate. Tax liabilities and high transaction costs due to frequent trading often results in poor long-term performance. In contrast, index funds just buy and hold stocks of companies in the S&P 500 index or some other index, so the cost for index funds is very low, as little as 1/20 the cost of an actively managed fund. There are numerous advantages that index funds have compared to playing the market, which is more like gambling.

In an index fund, not only are fees extremely low, but investors can sleep better and not worry about the vicissitudes of individual stocks or money managers. Compared to investing with active fund managers, index funds are less volatile, incur more predictable taxes, and are not prone to changes in managers or strategic direction. It is similar to investing in a gambling casino rather than playing at gaming tables. Through thick and thin, prosperity and depression, the stock market has risen an average of approximately 7.5 percent a year and bonds about 3.5 percent a year. Of course, gains or losses may differ widely depending on starting and ending dates. As an example, the S&P 500 gained a lofty 29.6 percent in 2013, an uncommonly good year.

Numerous studies, including one by the Financial Research Corporation and one by Vanguard, have shown that the most reliable predictor for future performance was that low-cost funds delivered an above average performance in all periods examined. In fact, the expense ratio was the most significant factor in determining the success of a fund. Hedge funds are a favorite investment vehicle managing an aggregate of three trillion dollars. The Bloomberg Global Aggregate Hedge Fund Index did worse than the S&P 500 Stock Index and the balanced portfolio of equities and bonds for six years in a row ending in 2014.

The power of compounding is the most important aspect of investing. Compounding is simply the act of making money on an investment or savings deposit that grows steadily through investment gains, dividends, and interest payments—basically earning money on money. For example, if you invest $10,000 in an index fund and the fund rises 10 percent in year one, the following year you will be making a gain on $11,000, not $10,000, and so on for successive years. Compounding is reminiscent of a parlay in which you win a bet and let the entire proceeds ride on the next bet. The difference between an investment and a parlay is in the parlay you lose everything if you lose either the first or second bet; in an investment you just keep compounding the initial investment plus interim gains or losses.

Earlier I talked about Ben Franklin, one of our country's founders, who invested money with a one hundred year horizon. A more recent example is the story of Rabbi Kripke and his wife Dorothy, long-time friends of Warren Buffett. Rabbi Kripke recently passed away, so this story became news. The Kripkes had a relatively small nest egg of $67,000, which they invested with Warren Buffett in the 1960s. Thirty years later, that investment grew to more than

$25,000,000, illustrating the power of compounding, albeit with critical assistance from one of the country's most famous investors.

A strategy of buying or saving and reinvesting gains (dividends or interest) on top of the original investment will reap the substantial benefits of compounding. It used to be that you could invest in a bank savings account and receive meaningful interest, but that has not been true in recent years. Interest rates have been close to zero so compounding has not been relevant in savings accounts. How times have changed. When Ronald Reagan was president, interest rates ballooned to 18 percent, and the inflation rate was high as well. There are alternative ways to eke out higher interest rates, such as certificates of deposit or Treasury bills. Whatever you do, as Ronald Reagan was famous for saying: "Stay the course." Compounding always works in the long term.

Overall, the best way to invest is through a combination of stocks and bonds. John Bogle believes that as you get older, you should lean increasingly toward bonds, even suggesting that the percentage of bonds in your portfolio should equate to your age. Bonds pay interest, which is beneficial to older people who need income for living expenses. Interest paid on municipal bonds issued by state and city governments are tax free to investors living in those jurisdictions. Younger investors are prone to taking chances and investing in high risk, high reward opportunities. The best recommendation is to invest a relatively small percentage of your money (say 10 percent or 20 percent) in riskier investments if you feel a passion for taking investment risks.

So there you have it. If you invest in index funds, you will not lose sleep over individual stock and bond investments, and your investments will likely grow at a compounded rate every year. You will have invested in the overall stock or bond market, which on average has experienced positive financial returns through good and bad times since the beginning of stock market indices.

Less worry, greater return—what more can you ask? The odds are with you, not against you, based on a track record of nearly one hundred years of financial history. A word of caution: if your investment is made at an inopportune time, i.e., just before a market crash, you will show a loss early on. But history shows that the loss will be reversed over time, particularly if you use "dollar cost averaging."

You may ask: If indexing is such a great concept why isn't everyone doing it, and what would happen if everyone did it? First of all, not everyone will do it. Second, despite the huge growth of index funds, they only account for 14 percent of the equity market and 3 percent of the fixed income market. Consequently, 86 percent of the equity market and 97 percent of the bond market involve active management. Incidentally, the extremely low cost of index funds mean they will only do a slight bit worse than the indexes they match, but do measurably better than managed funds that have substantially higher costs.

In the last decade a new investment vehicle has emerged called exchange-traded funds or ETFs for short. ETFs are similar to mutual funds, but are traded like stocks so that investors can track, sell, or buy at any time, as opposed to mutual funds, which are priced only at the close of day. ETF index funds, like their counterpart mutual funds, are low cost, do not have front loaded fees, and are growing rapidly in popularity. Currently, index mutual funds manage approximately $7 trillion, while ETF index funds total about $2 trillion. That gap will undoubtedly close as investors become more familiar with ETFs. In 2015 mutual funds, not index funds, will total about $13 trillion.

For excitement, it would be hard to beat investing as a venture capitalist or an angel investor. Angel groups have sprouted up across the country. Some cities have as many as five or ten angel groups. There are several hundred thousand angel investors. Some do not even realize they are categorized as angel investors. Angel investors invest in early stage companies known as start-ups. A typical angel investor may invest anywhere from $10,000 to $100,000 in a small company needing growth capital. It is common for early funding to come from friends, neighbors, doctors, and dentists.

If you have excess capital and would like to put some of your funds into emerging companies it is quite easy to join an angel group; you can find them listed on the Internet or you could educate yourself by reading several excellent books describing angel investing, such as *What Every Angel Investor Wants You To Know*, by Brian S. Cohen or *Angel Investing* by David S. Rose. Many retired executives have joined angel groups to lend their expertise and become involved in promising start-ups.

Accelerating the angel phenomenon is the recently passed Jobs Act that drastically lowered federal regulations for raising capital. An industry known as crowdsourcing has mushroomed to help individuals or small groups of people raise money for charity, ice cream shops, musical groups, restaurants, movies, etc. Crowdsourcing companies such as Kickstarter, GoFundMe, and Indiegogo have already raised hundreds of millions of dollars for entrepreneurs. In 2014 an estimated $5 billion will be raised from over 500 crowdsourcing platforms. A danger of raising money through crowdsourcing is that creative ideas are necessarily promulgated and can easily be copied.

The venture capital industry is composed of hundreds of venture capital funds that generally invest from $1 million to $50 million in companies further along than the ones of interest to angel groups. Investments in private companies usually start with common stock investments and then proceed to series A preferred stock, and sometimes all the way to a series H round. For successful companies, each round of investment is done at higher and higher prices. Companies that fail to perform do so-called "down and dirty rounds" at lower prices than before. The exit for VC investments is through outright sales to larger companies or by initial public offerings (IPOs). Payoffs can be very large in successful angel or venture capital investments, but the failure rate of individual investments is high. Nevertheless, it is possible for one investment to more than compensate for losses in an entire portfolio of ten or twenty companies. Be forewarned that there are very few investments that pay off as well as the stocks of Facebook, Google, or Apple, but payoffs of ten to one are entirely achievable.

In the 1990s major corporations launched in-house strategic venture capital funds when they saw that independent venture capital funds had high financial returns from investments in exciting companies. Corporate venturing has on the whole experienced positive results, strategically and financially, but some corporations have had problems because internal operating groups have not welcomed newer technologies that could make obsolete the technologies they are currently managing.

Investments in private companies are much more dangerous than investing in public companies. There is little oversight by the SEC or stock exchanges, and legal documentation is often not up to par. Boards of directors of private companies are generally composed more of investors than industry experts. Corporate governance is not polished and oversight may be wanting. Nonetheless, investors can learn a great deal by serving on boards of private companies and by interacting with management. From the time of initial investment to the time of exit from an investment, it can take as many as ten years, and I know of cases where it has taken fifteen to twenty years. Unlike investments in public stocks, there is little or no liquidity in private company investments.

If you cannot afford to wait ten years to get your money out, angel or venture capital investing may not be for you. By way of contrast, investors in public stocks have liquidity, quarterly financial reports, annual meetings, and a choice of 20,000 stocks to choose from in the United States alone. As mentioned previously, index funds provide a "safe harbor," which largely takes the risk out of investing in public stocks.

There is no equivalent safe harbor in the private sector. Management usually owns a majority of the company at early stages, so the board of directors may be more for show than oversight. An individual's allocation of funds is dependent on age, experience, and capital. Young people can take more chances because their best earnings years are ahead of them. Older people require more security and less risk. For those occupying the middle ground, it is best to save or invest on a regular basis ("dollar cost averaging"), certainly invest in public stocks, probably in bonds as well, and possibly invest 10 to 20 percent in private companies. One size does not fit all so it is best to get the advice of professional advisors, brokers, and planners before making major financial decisions.

Building wealth is not as important as living comfortably. I know something about building wealth, but there is a lot about finance that I do not know. There are experts in every nook and cranny of the wealth management business. There are experts in taxes, retirement, bonds, derivatives, insurance, foreign investments, unions, and so forth. In addition, there are experts in industries such as farming, industrials, technology, fine arts, precious metals, pharmaceuticals, health care, etc.

After all of my years in business, there is still a lot that I do not know. If you are an investor, or are seeking employment in a particular industry, it is best to find a mentor or a professional in the industry or specialty in which you have an interest. Many experts and union members have been certified by industry or occupational bodies that allow people to use letters after their name. This applies to industries such as insurance, money management, real estate, and jewelry, to mention a few. Occasionally a person becomes a standout in industry or business without benefit of a college degree or a designation after their name.

A broker is the closest that some investors ever get to real experts. Brokers are licensed by regulatory authorities and have wide knowledge in their particular industries, but they often depend on experts within their organizations for deeper knowledge. Investing is not easy, but the Internet is an excellent tool for beginning to gain knowledge about industries, companies, stocks, and brokers.

In this chapter I have given simple advice about managing money effectively. If you want to know more, there are many good books and classes to help you achieve a greater understanding of the markets and industries.

Afterword

IF YOU ARE ALREADY ENJOYING a life you find fulfilling, this book should inspire you to be happier and more productive. Hopefully, one or more of the four parts of this book struck a respondent cord with you. When I showed the draft of the book to two friends, the first replied that he loved it, but urged me to get rid of the chapter on math. The second replied that the math chapter was great and that his daughter loved all the math tricks and was already using them in school.

I have told you of my belief that happiness and excellent health begin with the right attitude, but in the complex society of today, to attain happiness you need to elevate your education by continually reading books and taking classes.

Working hard at being educated early in life pays dividends later in life. Even young children can learn very readily. For example, three-year-olds can learn to speak a language—any language. The brains of children are open to absorbing vast amounts of knowledge. And education is like compound interest—the more you know the more you can know. My book stresses speed in education because it is one thing to learn, but another to learn faster. Why read 200 words a minute when you can easily increase reading speed to 500 or even 1,000 words a minute? Learning speed math, improving memory, and developing excellent writing and speaking skills will help you lead a happier life with greater success.

I hope this book may help you find a higher level of employment consistent with current mores and technology. I have provided advice to make your life more exciting, to elevate your dreams, and to be eager to wake up in the morning to do something enjoyable.

I hope you will also find great happiness by helping others—especially your spouse, children, grandchildren, and friends. No matter how good or bad life is, you can always consider ways to improve yourself and help others if you think positively and do not get bogged down by negative thoughts.

It is unfortunately a fact of life that people who fail to save money and who make bad investment decisions are not likely to be very happy. I hope my advice about finances will help those people. In my lifetime I have used modern investment concepts such as compound interest, dollar cost averaging and investments in index funds to improve investment performance. I show statistically that if your money is passively managed in index funds rather than actively managed, the odds will shift in your favor so that you will be more successful and have less mental anguish.

Throughout the book I provided the "secrets" I utilized to improve my life and make me successful. I believe these secrets can also make you happier, healthier, smarter and more prosperous.

Please keep in mind my best advice:

▷ Think positively about everything

▷ Focus on solutions rather than problems

▷ Train your mind to always be happy

▷ Continually improve your education

▷ Get a better job if your current job is not interesting and fun

▷ Be confident

▷ Seek help if you have a lingering problem

As I have told you, I am also a great believer in *Parkinson's Law*, his explanation of how much time it takes to complete a task, which I paraphrase as "work takes up the time available." This is a very important law. I am sure that Parkinson would also agree with the well-known saying "do not put off till tomorrow what you can do today."

Most of all, it is important to understand that by constantly improving your education, your mind is opened to great ideas that you may never before have thought about. You do not know how powerful you can be until you get involved in learning something new. It is not about who you know but what you ***do not know***. Expand your brain cells and heed the following advice.

Unless you take an online or in-person course in speed-reading ***you do not know*** how fast you can read.

Unless you learn a simple system to remember twenty things in any order ***you do not know*** that you can throw away shopping lists, speech notes and the like.

Unless you take on a new hobby ***you do not know*** that you can become one of the foremost experts in that hobby.

Unless you can give a one-minute speech without notes ***you do not know*** that you can give longer speeches without notes.

Unless you invest a little bit every month ***you do not know*** how dollar cost averaging and compound interest can increase your savings to a large amount in ten or twenty years.

Unless you have confidence *you do not know* how to succeed.

Unless you show love to your family, friends, and important others, *you do not know* how much love you will get back in return.

You do not know how happy you can be until you try.

Notes

1 Evelyn Schuckburg, translation, *Ancient History Sourcebook: Cicero (105– 43 BCE): Old Age, c. 65 BCE*. Fordham University: www.fordham.edu/halsall/ancient/cicero-oldage.asp.

2 Kathy LaTour, "Power of Placebo Effect," Cure Today, http://www.curetoday.com/publications/cure/2014/fall2014/ Power-of-Placebo-Effect.

3 David Cameron, "Placebos Work—Even Without Deception." *HARVARD Gazette*, December 22, 2010, http://news.harvard.edu/gazette/story/2010/12/placebos-work-%E2%80%94-even-without-deception/.

4 Brian Reid, "The Nocebo Effect: Placebo's Evil Twin." April 29, 2002, http://www.curezone.org/art/read.asp?ID=142&db=1&C0=14.

5 Paul Enck, "Beware the Nocebo Effect." *The New York Times*, August 10, 2012.

6 Irving Kirsch, "Challenging Received Wisdom: Antidepressants and the Placebo Effect." *McGill Journal of Medicine* (Nov 2008; 11(2) 219-222).

7 Peter Arguriou, "The Placebo Effect." Extracted from *Nexus Magazine*, Volume 14, Number 4 (June–July 2007), from *Nexus Magazine* website.

8 Helen Pilcher, "The Science of Voodoo: When Mind Attacks Body." *New Scientist Health,* issue 2708 (May 13, 2009).

9 Arguriou, "The Placebo Effect."

Acknowledgments

I WOULD LIKE TO ACKNOWLEDGE THE EFFORTS and encouragement of a number of people who helped with this book. First, I would like to thank my researcher and administrative assistant, Jan Starbird-Veltidi. Without her efforts I would never have been able to write this book. A special thanks to five people who read the manuscript and encouraged me to complete the book. They are John Allen, Robert Gambee, Robert Reese, Lucia Kaiser, and, last but not least, Judy Katz. Thanks to my wife, Jonelle, and my children Vance, Valerie, and Lianna, and their spouses and children for allowing me the time to write the book. A final thanks to my agent, Bill Gladstone of Waterside Productions and to my publisher, Kenzi, and Nancy Sugihara of SelectBooks. Finally, thanks to all the people I wrote about in the book. You know who you are.